On Christology, Anthropology, Cognitive Science and the Human Body

READING AUGUSTINE

Series Editor:
Miles Hollingworth

Reading Augustine presents books that offer personal, nuanced and oftentimes literary readings of Saint Augustine of Hippo. Each time, the idea is to treat Augustine as a spiritual and intellectual icon of the Western tradition, and to read through him to some or other pressing concern of our current day, or to some enduring issue or theme. In this way, the writers follow the model of Augustine himself, who produced his famous output of words and ideas in active tussle with the world in which he lived. When the series launched, this approach could raise eyebrows, but now that technology and pandemics have brought us into the world and society like never before, and when scholarship is expected to live the same way and responsibly, the series is well-set and thriving.

Volumes in the series:

On Music, Sense, Affect, and Voice, Carol Harrison
On Solitude, Conscience, Love and Our Inner, and Outer Lives, Ron Haflidson
On Creation, Science, Disenchantment, and the Contours of Being and Knowing, Matthew W. Knotts
On Agamben, Arendt, Christianity, and the Dark Arts of Civilization, Peter Iver Kaufman
On Self-Harm, Narcissism, Atonement, and the Vulnerable Christ, David Vincent Meconi
On Faith, Works, Eternity, and the Creatures We Are, André Barbera
On Time, Change, History, and Conversion, Sean Hannan
On Compassion, Healing, Suffering, and the Purpose of the Emotional Life, Susan Wessel
On Consumer Culture, Identity, the Church and the Rhetorics of Delight, Mark Clavier
On Creativity, Liberty, Love and the Beauty of the Law, Todd Breyfogle
On Education, Formation, Citizenship and the Lost Purpose of Learning, Joseph Clair
On Ethics, Politics and Psychology in the Twenty-First Century, John Rist
On God, the Soul, Evil and the Rise of Christianity, John Peter Kenney
On Love, Confession, Surrender and the Moral Self, Ian Clausen
On Memory, Marriage, Tears, and Meditation, Margaret R. Miles
On Mystery, Ineffability, Silence, and Musical Symbolism, Laurence Wuidar

On Christology, Anthropology, Cognitive Science and the Human Body

Martin Claes

LONDON • NEW YORK • OXFORD • NEW DELHI • SYDNEY

T&T CLARK
Bloomsbury Publishing Plc
50 Bedford Square, London, WC1B 3DP, UK
1385 Broadway, New York, NY 10018, USA
29 Earlsfort Terrace, Dublin 2, Ireland

BLOOMSBURY, T&T CLARK and the T&T Clark logo are trademarks of
Bloomsbury Publishing Plc

First published in Great Britain 2022

Cover image: *Vitruvian Man*, Leonardo Da Vinci, circa 1490.
Historical Images Archive / Alamy Stock Photo

A catalogue record for this book is available from the British Library.

Library of Congress Cataloging-in-Publication Data
Names: Claes, Martin, author.
Title: On Christology, anthropology, cognitive science and the human body /
Martin Claes.
Description: London ; New York : T&T Clark, 2022. | Series: Reading Augustine |
Includes bibliographical references and index. | Identifiers: LCCN 2021041864
(print) | LCCN 2021041865 (ebook) | ISBN 9781350296084 (pb) | ISBN
9781350296091 (hb) | ISBN 9781350296107 (epdf) | ISBN 9781350296114 (epub)
Subjects: LCSH: Human body—Religious aspects—Christianity. | Incarnation. |
Philosophical theology. | Augustine, of Hippo, Saint, 354-430.
Classification: LCC BT741.3 .C527 2022 (print) | LCC BT741.3 (ebook) | DDC 233/.5–dc23
LC record available at https://lccn.loc.gov/2021041864
LC ebook record available at https://lccn.loc.gov/2021041865.

ISBN: HB: 978-1-3502-9609-1
PB: 978-1-3502-9608-4
ePDF: 978-1-3502-9610-7
ePUB: 978-1-3502-9611-4

Series: Reading Augustine

Typeset by Deanta Global Publishing Services, Chennai, India
Printed and bound in Great Britain

To find out more about our authors and books visit www.bloomsbury.com and
sign up for our newsletters.

CONTENTS

PREFACE

Reason: Entreat of God health and help, that you may the better compass your desires, and commit to writing this very petition, that you may be the more courageous in the offspring of your brain. Then, what you discover sum up in a few brief conclusions.

(*SOLILOQUIES*, I.1, TRANSL. C. C. STARBUCK, 1888 NPNF, VOL. 7)

Augustine was about to inquire the self and the chief good in dialogue with Reason in the *Soliloquies*. His conversation was with Reason in the self. The dialogue in this book is directed externally but centres on manifestations of bodily selves. Hence, this book recognizes multiplicity of centres. Though, they unite in their reflections on the person of Christ.

Courage and offspring of the brain: writing a book on Augustine in interdisciplinary context requires courage. It requires even more humility in confrontation with the vast amount of labour from colleagues in scholarship who have devoted their best capacities and energy to make their insights accessible.

Though, humility does not make speechless. It polishes words in sentences and makes conscious that many may have better insights. However, dialogue respects the dynamic of statements and the rebuttal of these. It is this type of dialogue I have aimed for in this project. I see it as an invitation for future conversations in respect and friendship.

ACKNOWLEDGEMENTS

Writing a book is a work of solidarity in solitude. Many have shared in the unity of love and friendship which accompanied the years I have worked on this project. Many have made their contributions in a multitude of forms. Shared experiences, such as hospitality, exchange of ideas in mutual respect between colleagues in parish and university and support of dear friends in The Hague, my parish and many other places, have enabled me to carry on this endeavour.

A special word of acknowledgement for staff and colleagues of Tilburg School of Catholic Theology at Tilburg University: They offered the conditions that made it possible to complete this book. Augustinians and research on Augustine are a favourable combination. Hence, I express my greatest gratitude towards the Dutch province of Augustinians for spiritual and material aid and towards the Belgium province of Augustinians for their hospitality and support in the Augustijns Historisch Instituut in Heverlee. Another word of gratitude for Anthony Dupont from KU Leuven. Contagious energy and a shared passion for the bishop of Hippo were the constituents for friendship in a brotherhood of scholarship.

A researcher does not work without the aid of many professionals from the community in and around the university. Thanks to Mark Vitullo for his kind and expert advice on writing a book. I am grateful to my colleagues of the Centre for the Study of Early Christianity and my former promoters Willemien Otten and Paul van Geest. My gratitude goes to Michael Cameron (Portland) and Aku Visala (Helsinki) for their encouraging advice at the beginning of this project. As a pastor in a parish, I owe much to the experience of day-to-day life in a diocesan setting. Therefore, I express gratitude to my bishop mgr. Gerard de Korte for entrusting me with the combination of pastoral and academic work, and for continuing support for further research.

Over the years I have appreciated very much the work and patient attention of Miles Hollingworth as a responsible and skilful editor of this series, and I want to express gratitude to the editorial staff from the theology department at Bloomsbury Publishers.

Finally, a word of thanks for the patience of my friends and family. They themselves know best how vital their contributions were in this project: often from a distance, but never in absence.

ABBREVIATIONS

Works of Augustine

HL   *On the Happy Life (De beata vita)*, Translation,
Annotation, and Commentary by Michael P. Foley,
St. Augustine's Cassiciacum Dialogues, Volume 2,
Yale University Press 2019.

GM   *On Genesis against the Manicheans (De Genesi
adversus Manichaeos)*, transl. Edmund Hill: 'On
Genesis: A Refutation of the Manichees' in *The Works
of Saint Augustine: A Translation for the 21st Century*,
Vol. I/13, New York: New City Press 1991.

Conf   *Confessions (Confessiones)*, transl. E. B. Pusey, in
The Confessions of St. Augustine, Waiheke Island:
Floating Press 1921.

Trin   *On Trinity (De Trinitate)*, transl. Edmund Hill,
The Trinity, in *The Works of Saint Augustine:
A Translation for the 21st Century*, Vol. I/5,
New York: New City Press 1991.

CG   *The City of God (De civitate Dei)* transl. by Gerald
G. Walsh, S. J. and Daniel J. Honan *The City of God*.
Books I–XXII, Washington, D.C.: Catholic University
of America Press, 2008.

Others

NRSVCE   *The Holy Bible, New Revised Standard Version
Catholic Edition*, Division of Christian Education of
the National Council of the Churches of Christ in the
United States of America, 1965.

1

Introduction

1.1 No unity without struggle: No struggle without unity?

Today's world is observed within a disenchanting efficiency. The marvel of real- or near real-time communication shows us a Notre Dame Cathedral in flames. Horrific acts of terrorism can be watched in all their direct impact. This change in communication has its consequences: diversity, multiplicity and flexibility have made fluid almost everything that matters. Yet, at the same time, under the surface of this complexity looms a desire for unity, simplicity or even oneness. For many of us, these perspectives of multiplicity in communication have shaped our lives and offer the necessary precondition of freedom to develop and express our personal talents and aims in life. This can make people happy. This is the freedom that also enriches my personal life.

However, there are many phenomena which can be observed that indicate that this multiplicity has its limits in the context of the unfolding of human talents. This maximum for multiplicity regards human capacity to focus attention in depth and in perception. Now, in the midst of the turmoil of sense impressions of daily life, many people seek unity and agreement in personal contact. Therefore, they build mini-communities on social media, blogs, internet magazines and so on. Additionally, in real life most individuals live in circles of family ties, friends, work and recreation. However, that these communities in reality often reflect the tensions and divisions of society seldom completely supresses the desire for unity, community and oneness. I am a participant in several of these communities: village, family, university and church. No unity without struggle. No struggle without unity. In his era, Augustine expressed his concerns on unity in the daily life of a Christian community more than once in his controversy with the Donatists. His comments not only have been relevant for theologians but have also influenced politicians and leaders of states.

Yet, unity, oneness or even simplicity have never signalled easy roads in intellectual discourse or popular communication. Characterized as a secular age (Charles Taylor), this twenty-first century presents in the midst of a high of ratio and empiricism some nasty irrational traits: terrorism, religious fundamentalism, ecological crisis, climatological changes and recently a virus outbreak. Buffered selves have become efficient in convincing other buffered selves of their perverse logic that leads to the neglect of the unity between humankind and ecological environment. Others seek unity in exegesis of religious texts and praxis.

The latter type of unity offers for many people fundaments for their lives. Religions have been explained by anthropologists as important organizing systems within society (Clifford Geertz, Armin Geertz). However, when this unity closes and evolves into ideology or even fundamentalism, it can manifest itself as an illusion of unity. From adolescence on, I have sought my source of unity within a tradition of faith, especially in its compelling manifestations in music and monastic life. I have been fascinated since then by the healing tensions between oneness and diversity. I find these reflected in the narratives on the person of Christ. Yet, this same tradition has suffered from the wounds of division. Augustine, on his turn, was in a steady dialogue with non-Christian or non-orthodox authors and groups. He presented Christ as a biblical unifier in his mystical concept of the whole body of Christ: *totus Christus*.

1.1.1 The human body as a manifestation of unity?

Within the variety of opinions and reflections on unity and diversity, the most evident manifestation of the topic of unity is the human body. Since every human person exists within the integrity of his body, this embodied existence creates an existential bond between all persons. This bond includes the deceased persons in the consequences of their past, presence and thought. Future people are included as an intellectual space of hope. Personalities from the past project the framework for theological and philosophical reflection. Influential persons, such as Augustine, have created intellectual resources for human development in the reflection on its proper position in the world and the cosmos. The framework of my vision on the human body is formed not only by its daily existence but also by Augustine's testimonial of human bodily embeddedness within the spiritual body of Christ. But how corporeal is this spiritual body?

For Augustine, in his era, it was not extremely difficult to argue in concordance with Paul in his *The City of God* that every human person will rise in a new type of bodily existence (*corpus spiritale*) after this life. However, in the twenty-first century, although the topic of the logical possibility of a physical resurrection recently has been studied by philosophers such as Trenton Merricks (physicalist) and Richard Swinburne (dualist), neither public opinion nor academic discussions on the human body have been dominated by religious opinions and theories. In the recent past, an exception is to be found in a negative sense: child abuse within a variety of settings including church and religious groups. Therefore, in some countries, religious opinions on moral topics initiate temporary social discussion (abortion, prostitution etc.), but rarely succeed in contributing to a positive sense to public discourse on the human body and on humanity. A serious crisis in the communication of theology and of communication of faith in Christian churches and other religious groups is noticed. Yet in my life in pastoral service and in academic dialogue, I see how patristic theology has faced many questions on unity and diversity that matter. Many of these matters ask for an answer of 'why' questions, rather than on 'how' questions. The latter have been answered extensively in the natural and cognitive sciences. The former was the domain of literary interpretation, hermeneutical methods and of philosophy and theology.

1.1.2 Brainwaves on unity and the human body in early Christian theology, cognitive sciences, philosophical theology and biology: Are they methodological monsters?

These relevant questions from early Christian theology regard, for example, the human body in its potential in the process of healing.

Despite the variety of anthropological theories among patristic authors on the human soul in its complex relationship with the human body, no author denied that it is in an embodied period of life that human persons grow and develop in physical, intellectual and spiritual sense. For Augustine, healing is fundamentally related to restoration of unity within the temporal state of dispersion. Christ was his model as One in God and in diversity for the needs of humankind. Although faith in bodily resurrection of Christ has not been dominating public debates, the topic it expresses – embodied life and its potential unity after death – still incites the quest for perfection and healing and appeals to the thoughts and concerns of the many.

Similarly, in the second half of the last century empirical sciences, such as the cognitive sciences and natural sciences, discovered the study of religions and religious behaviour as an indispensable part of their research, in particular studies related to human well-being and anthropology. Many publications on the embodied effects of religion and religious behaviour on human persons and groups have been made since then. These regard not only theories on the development and function of religions within the micro-context of the development of the human brain but also socio-cultural effects of religions and religious behaviour on the macro-level in society and politics.

Yet, theologians such as Augustine did not share the naturalistic emphasis of their methods. Except for some treatises which found their initiative in the practicalities of pastorate (e.g. *The First Catechetical Instruction, On the Care of the Dead*), Augustine focussed, in his reflection, on the human relationship of faith with God. The diversity of topics he discussed on biblical exegesis was in the context of the Nicene and post-Nicene theology. The model for the human relationship with God was Christ in his scriptural and dogmatic shape. The sacramental and pastoral life of the Church of Northern Africa has been the setting of Augustine's written work.

Since many intellectually well-versed people in society and academy no longer self-evidently share the narratives and characteristic patterns of argumentation and organization, the contribution of theology in contemporary discourse on global problems is no longer manifest. From the academic perspective, a division has been suggested between confessional theology and scholarly study of religion that meets the standard of naturalistic science in method. Early Christian studies have included not only scholarly methods from philology, archaeology, history and cultural sciences in order to describe and explain early Christian texts in its cultural and historical context in synchrony but also the genesis of certain philosophical or theological *topoi* in diachronic perspective.

Apart from the unavoidable link between historical and systematic approaches in research on early Christian texts, it is in diachronic research that knowledge of the theological content of early Christian theological reflection is most necessary. It is this diachronic thematic research which has been influential in the philosophical discussions on poverty, climate changes and terrorism.

Patristic theology evidently cannot provide direct answers to these questions. However, it can inspire contemporary discourse with its wealth of narratives from a diverse society in which a Christian minority developed towards a state religion. Since patristic theology interprets and re-interprets testimonials and treatises of early Christian theologians in the light of new historical and philological evidence and insights, a renewed dialogue between contemporary research questions and early Christian theological texts appears to be most welcome, especially regarding anthropological topics.

Since theology has demonstrated to be capable in periods of crises (early Christian debates on Christology, Reformation, etc.) to resuscitate its potential to renew itself, I will explore in this book possibilities for a theological experiment to read Augustine, focussed on unity and the human body. For this vision on unity, I will turn to contemporary discussions on bodily unity within philosophical theology, cognitive science of religion (CSR) and biology.

1.1.3 Can a dialogue of hospitality be successful?

In the end, early Christian discourse on the human body was inextricably connected with a vast mass of complex details related to debates on the person and nature of Christ as a human *and* divine Son of God. As early Christian theologians have not limited their inspiration to biblical scripture alone, the twenty-first-century separation between the disciplines of theology and philosophy was not obvious or broadly defended. Patristic theologians were eager to integrate philosophical concepts in their discourse in order to be able to give a rational foundation to their religious convictions and beliefs. As Pierre Hadot has argued in his book *Philosophy as a Way of Life*, philosophy included elements which are characterized as religious (mysticism) in our ages. Therefore, early Christian and late-antique religions seldom were completely separated from rational philosophical discourse.

A new approach to the topic of unity and the human body in the context of cognitive sciences, philosophical theology and biology in confrontation with early Christian theology, accordingly, requires a dialogue of hospitality. Hospitality, in this case, presupposes respect for the peculiar methods of the respective disciplines. It asks also to respect the differences in methodology of the disciplines involved. In the experiment of dialogue that follows, I have been inspired by the invitation of Armin Geertz to scholars of religion. In his *Cognitive Approaches to the Study of Religion*, he asks attention to the relevance of developments in cognitive sciences for the study of religion. In his polemic on Daniel Dennett's treatise of scholarly reflections in CSR, Geertz points out that a more embodied view on religion is necessary. Thus, justice can be done to relevant results from neurophysiology, evolutionary biology, anthropology and psychology. His invitation explicitly includes theologians.

A different approach has been offered by Ilkka Pyysiäinen in his book *How Religion Works: Towards a New Cognitive Science of Religion* (2003). He argued that a specific cognitive domain for religion presumably does not exist. In his view, religion is 'a category of thoughts and behaviours based on quite ordinary cognitive mechanisms'. Yet, he focussed on counter-intuitive agents and their representation that are shared by a group of people which they believe to be true. Therefore, scientific study of religion in this view has the selection of these counter-intuitive representations as objects of belief as its special aim. The focus of theoretical comparative religion is consequentially on the theories on religious phenomena and their development, while applied comparative religion focuses on the religious phenomena themselves in the context of these theories.

Another inspiration for the project of this book was Aku Visala's critique on methodology in CSR in his book *Naturalism, Theism and the Cognitive Study of Religion: Religion Explained* from 2011. In this book Visala proposes a methodological pluralism in the study of religion. The first part of his book argues that in its empiricist methodology, the cognitive sciences in their epistemology have simultaneously introduced a one-sided naturalistic focus on the *explanandum* in research (how-questions). In his view, a discipline such as theology can create contrast spaces in the process of research in its ability to answer why-questions. It is in these specific methodological concerns that I see a promising contribution for patristic theology, especially Augustine's impact on the discussion of the human body and unity. This relates in Augustine's written work to his reflections on Christ and his direct- and indirect (sacramental) unifying action and presence within Christian communities.

1.1.4 How does a threefold Christological perspective of kenosis, *Logos-Sarx* and resurrection empower dialogue with philosophical theology?

From the perspective of philosophy, a minority of scholars studied major topics from Christian doctrine. Their aim has been to reflect on the confrontation between analytic philosophy and the theologian's discourse on Trinity, Christ, resurrection and the afterlife. In the end, these scholarly debates sometimes have had their effects on popular apologetics (Richard Swinburne in apologetic Roman Catholic media). Nevertheless, their proper intention generally has been to reflect on the main topics of Christian doctrine from contemporary philosophical perspective. Current debate concentrates mainly on the position and person of Christ. In the context of the discourse on unity and the human body to be followed in this book, I will concentrate on three types of Christological perspectives: kenotic, *Logos-Sarx* Christology and, lastly, the aspect of the body in the resurrection. They will guide a reading of a selection of Augustine's work on the topic of the human body, exemplified in his reflections on the body of Christ. They also reflect the fundamental lines of salvation history: incarnation – unifying activity of the Word in the flesh, resurrection and perfection.

Philosophers who concentrate on the kenotic perspective on Christ generally stress the self-emptying act of God in taking a human body in Jesus. Hence, their discussions on unity within the person of Christ often have focussed on the concept of omnipotence and on communication between the divine and the human mind. Consequently, a two-mind hypothesis developed. Philosophers who have focussed on classical *Logos-Sarx* Christology generally adhere a dualistic anthropology. This enabled them to reflect in a consistent mode on the two natures within the person of Christ. Critics of this strain within philosophical theology have referred to an observed tendency to maintain a hidden form of idealism/ monism. Consequentially, the essence of the human person is described as immaterial and disembodied. Physicalist philosophy has been studying among others the embodied state of Christ in the resurrection. They conclude that the Christian doctrine of bodily resurrection is to be defended only under the presupposition of a physicalist anthropology (Trenton Merricks).

Recent scholarly work in philosophical theology (Rea and Flint 2009) discusses, with the help of analytic philosophical concepts and tools, comments and analyses of the aforementioned major topics in Christian doctrine. However, many of these discussions revolve around the hovering topic of unity. This involves unity within the Trinity, unity within the person of Christ, unity of the human person in embodied temporal existence and, lastly, unity in the resurrection.

1.1.5 Augustine on unity in Christ: A patristic road to new speech in theology?

Augustine in most cases expressed his ideas on anthropology in the context of reflections on the person of Christ within the Trinity and in his embodied human shape. Unity is his favourite concept. It provided Augustine with a pivotal idea that enabled him to explain a complex theological concept as incarnation. Augustine's proper contribution in this discussion on the human body of Christ was not delivered as an extended number of explicit references to the human body of Christ. Elsewhere, I have argued that despite Van Bavel's sharp observation of the scarcity of these texts, Augustine's presentation of a bodily presence and action of Christ is shaped by an accent on the worthiness of the human body as a place for and of salvation: *locus salvandi*. Reasons are likely to be found in Augustine's reaction to Manichean negative evaluation of the human body and in its place in creation. Additionally, this relatively strong corporeal feature of Augustine's anthropology was discussed in a homiletic context with the help of sacramental metaphors. It is principally the balance within Augustine's Christology which has brought him the reputation of a forerunner of the Chalcedonian definition of one person in two natures: divine and human.

Although it has happened that theologians evaluated Augustine's Christology in the shadow of the Chalcedonian council as 'not very special or significant', I invite the reader to participate in the experiment to read specimens of Augustine's insights in dialogue with the perspective of unity and the human body in contemporary philosophical theology and cognitive sciences. Even though the significance of the person of Christ is no longer evident in contemporary discourse on unity and diversity, I envisage that Augustine's careful argumentations can provide inspiration and significant narrative. This endeavour may incite renewed dialogue between theology and other disciplines. The result will be a re-reading of Augustine's anthropology.

1.1.6 The Body of Christ: A human body?

Discussion on the human body in modern Christology found its initiatives among others in a growing attention in anthropology and CSR for the embodied condition of humanity. This discourse was boosted by the influence of feminist theories and gender-oriented methods in social sciences. Theology of liberation pointed to the dominating role of the body in the submission of minorities (black, gay, lesbian rights). Yet, reflection on the unity within the human person remained relatively scarce and, with exception of Michel Foucault, early Christian sources were often neglected.

The bodily state of Christ as a suffering man has become a model for the suppressed and people in misery. Marilyn McCord Adams has made this sorrowful Christ the point of departure for her *Christ and Horrors* theology. She has recovered St. Thomas Aquinas as the foundation of her kenotic theology. The latter describes an omnipotent God who becomes the slave to a suffering race of humankind, as they participated in the horrors of human existence. In Chapter 3, I will ask attention to her theology of the body of Christ within the section on kenotic Christology.

In dualistic and idealistic anthropology, the discussion on the role and necessity of the human body of Christ is dominating. Critics of this view have been concerned on the depth and relevance of Christ's embodied life. Not only Johannine theology but also aspects of Neoplatonism and Christology have proved to be compatible with aspects of orthodox Christianity (Stephen T. Davis).

Most of the authors within philosophical anthropology, and philosophy of mind and consciousness, adheres to physicalist theories. Within this niche of research, a wide variety of theories explain sensorial and intellectual phenomena with the assistance of the supervenience principle. Fundamental is the assumption that eventual non-bodily intellectual or sensory entities supervene on their material matrix, the brain. Many theories have in common that scholars recognize the existence of sensorial and intellectual phenomena but disagree on the ontological status of the latter. Strict physicalism situates all activities related to consciousness within the brain in its biological structures. Trenton Merricks, a known physicalist, denies in his metaphysics the existence of things, but acknowledges 'simples arranged to look like objects'. Nevertheless, Merricks designed a physicalist Christology and focussed in his article 'The Resurrection of the Body' (Rea and Flint 2009, 476) on the how and why of bodily resurrection. Although currently a nihilist, Merricks includes the human person in his metaphysics. I will return to his work in Chapter 3 in the section on the resurrection and perfection

1.2 Can three perspectives on Christ enable a dialogue between Augustine and philosophical theology?

1.2.1 Christ in kenosis: A divine slave in human body?

Kenotic Christology has deep roots in Pauline biblical thought. It is focussed on the self-emptying act of God in the taking of a human body. Not only 'slave', 'servant', 'obedience' but also 'exaltation' and 'glorification' are keywords of Paul's poetic description of God's descendance in the humanity of Christ. Augustine's fascination with the topic of incarnation led him more than once to favourite verses from Phil. 2.5-11. Not only Christ's humility but also Paul's formulation of Christ being human 'in the form of God' *(in forma Dei)* provided Augustine with the necessary scriptural footing for his digressions on the person of Christ in his sermons and exegetic treatises. Most of these Christological reflections bear the traces of Augustine's deep roots in Nicene theology. The latter had its special focus on the aspect of unity between the divine persons, and found its expression in the frequency of Augustine's quotes of Phil. 2.6: *in forma Dei* (more than 345 times in the oeuvre of Augustine).

Paul's hymn on Christ exhibits in its context of a pastoral exhortation a theological attitude of humility in combination with exaltation and glorification.

Let the same mind be in you that was in Christ Jesus,

who, though he was in the form of God,
did not regard equality with God
as something to be exploited,
but emptied himself,
taking the form of a slave,
being born in human likeness.
And being found in human form,
he humbled himself
and became obedient to the point of death –
even death on a cross.

Therefore God also highly exalted him
and gave him the name
that is above every name,
so that at the name of Jesus
every knee should bend,
in heaven and on earth and under the earth,
and every tongue should confess
that Jesus Christ is Lord,
to the glory of God the Father.

(*NRSVCE*: PHIL 2.5-11)

Since Paul's poem on God's salvific action in Christ included both a descending (incarnation) and an ascending (glorification) *impetus,* this fragment of Phil. was fitting very well in Augustine's need to demonstrate scriptural roots for divine unity, even while God was human in Christ.

In Chapter 2, three Augustinian texts are discussed regarding the topic of unity and the human body. The context is Augustine's Christology. In the first text from *On Genesis against the Manicheans* II.24.37 (*De Genesi adversus Manichaeos*), henceforth *GM,* Augustine elaborates on the human body in the exegesis of Gen. 2.24: 'For this reason, a man shall leave father and mother and stick to his wife; and they shall be two in one flesh.' Augustine's exegesis focusses on the complex process of incarnation in the relationship of Christ and the Church. His intention is to demonstrate that God was not materially depicted in the book of Genesis, as has been the contention of the Manichees. In Augustine's view, God's nature was not material. He was not in any way absent or wanting, while human in Christ. The process which leads Christians to perceive gradually the Word within the human Jesus is adapted to the needs of humanity's limited capacities. Paul's kenotic hymn on Christ helped him to explain how God's self-emptying act in Christ is compared perfectly to human vulnerability.

A second text that will be discussed is Phil. 2.5-11 from *On Trinity* II.1-5.9. In this second book of *On Trinity* (*Trin*), Augustine studied theophanies as described in the Bible (Abraham, Moses, Daniel). Against gnostic and Manichean groups, he maintained his idea on the invisibility of God. He discussed these biblical topics in the context of a debate on the unity of the divine persons in the aftermath of the Nicene council. Augustine's reflections on the person of Christ exhibit a remarkable balance between Johannine Word Christology (I and the Father are one) and kenotic accent on the salvific action of the human Christ. The latter includes the domain of corporeality and the human body. For Augustine the sphere of the sensory was situated in the Christian life of the faithful. Its humility makes it accessible for all. Its divine origen (creation) fits human weakness. The verses of Phil. 2.5-11 provided Augustine with a scriptural foundation for his contention that despite the corporeal state of the human body of Christ (*forma servi*), unity persisted within the three divine persons of Trinity.

Modern kenotic Christology has engaged in the debate on the person of Christ around the divine concepts of unity, theodicy and omnipotence. Since Christ took the form of a slave and was born in human likeness, scholars have debated on the (lack of) omnipotence of the human Jesus. In this kenotic context Marilyn McCord Adams' comments on Augustine are going to be studied further on, in dialogue with Augustine's *On Genesis against the Manicheans*. Creation and the role of Christ as the new Adam is a basic concept in Augustine's exposé on omnipotence. In the course of this book, the concept of unity in Augustine's *Logos-Sarx* Christology will be examined in the context of the publications of Stephen Davis and a contrasting theory of Thomas Morris. Lastly, Trenton Merricks' 'The Resurrection of the Body' (Rea and Flint 2009, 476) stipulates the topic of resurrection and the human body. It will be read in dialogue with Augustine's *The City of God*.

1.2.2 Christ in incarnation: The divine Word in human flesh?

Augustine's view on the person of Christ has been influenced by the reading of the *libri platonicorum* and by Johannine theology of the Word. The exegesis of the Johannine prologue on the mission of the Word frequently illuminated the account of creation from the book of Genesis. The latter was of great importance for Augustine in the context of his polemics with Manichean and gnostic groups. Both have disputed Genesis' story of creation. In their eyes, the creation of material reality did not go in harmony with an immaterial concept of God. Manichees even stipulated material features of God, such as hairs and nails. In *Confessions* VII.9.13-14, Augustine discussed the topic of humanity in the setting of humility and Platonist pride. At this place in *Confessions* (*Conf*), he explicitly states that he read in these platonic books John's theology:

> And Thou, willing first to show me how Thou resistest the proud, but givest grace unto the humble, and by how great an act of Thy mercy Thou hadst traced out to men the way of humility, in that Thy Word was made flesh, and dwelt among men: – Thou procuredst for me, by means of one puffed up with

most unnatural pride, certain books of the Platonists, translated
from Greek into Latin. And therein I read, not indeed in the
very words, but to the very same purpose, enforced by many
and divers reasons, that in the beginning was the Word, and the
Word was with God, and the Word was God. (*Conf* VII.9.13,
transl. Pusey)

The prologue of John's Gospel (Jn 1.1-18) served for Augustine
as a key text in his anthropology and view on the human body.
However, in most cases, a reference to the previously mentioned
Pauline Christology is never far away in the text. Both theological
extremes create in Augustine's theological reflection a well-balanced
account of incarnation and salvation that made him the forerunner
in Chalcedonian Christology.

In the beginning was the Word, and the Word was with God,
and the Word was God. He was in the beginning with God. All
things came into being through him, and without him not one
thing came into being. What has come into being in him was life,
and the life was the light of all people. The light shines in the
darkness, and the darkness did not overcome it.

There was a man sent from God, whose name was John. He
came as a witness to testify to the light, so that all might believe
through him. He himself was not the light, but he came to testify
to the light. The true light, which enlightens everyone, was
coming into the world.

He was in the world, and the world came into being through
him; yet the world did not know him. He came to what was
his own, and his own people did not accept him. But to all who
received him, who believed in his name, he gave power to become
children of God, who were born, not of blood or of the will of
the flesh or of the will of man, but of God.

And the Word became flesh and lived among us, and we have
seen his glory, the glory as of a father's only son, full of grace
and truth. (John testified to him and cried out, 'This was he of
whom I said, 'He who comes after me ranks ahead of me because
he was before me.') From his fullness we have all received, grace

upon grace. The law indeed was given through Moses; grace and truth came through Jesus Christ. No one has ever seen God. It is God the only Son, who is close to the Father's heart, who has made him known. (*NRSVCE*: Phil 2.5-11)

Yet, this common ground between Augustine and the platonic books read was evaluated with ambivalence in his *Confessions*. After a statement on resemblances between Platonic thought and Johannine theology of the Word, Augustine referred to Christ's humility. The hidden wisdom for the wise was revealed to babes: the unlearned Christian faithful. As the teachers of sublime platonic teaching did not recognize the voice of the humble Christ who said: 'Learn of me, that I am meek and humble of heart' (Mt. 11.29), Platonism failed to recognize the human Christ as the Word. This made them fools in Augustine's perception while professing that they were wise (*Conf* VII.9.14).

Philosophical reflection on these aspects of Christian doctrine has up until now mainly focussed on the relationship between Jesus the Word and the overarching process of incarnation. This debate has found its results in a variety of theories on Trinity. These theories deliberate among others on an apparent logical enigma: How can God be simultaneously one and three divine persons? Thomas Morris' *The Logic of God Incarnate* (2001) is a fine specimen of a recent defence of this aspect of Christian doctrine in the perspective of analytic philosophy. Richard Swinburne's book *The Christian God* (1994) attracted much scholarly and public attention when he concluded that Christian doctrine is a probable and defendable philosophical option. However, its dualistic anthropology was criticized for its neglect of the embodied state of Christ. I will return to these authors in Chapter 3.

1.2.3 Christ in resurrection: The model of human embodiment?

The topic of the resurrection was for Augustine inextricably related to the bodily resurrection of Christ. Under influence of Paul's epistle to the Romans, Augustine was convinced that not only Christ but all humans are destined to be perfected to conform to the image of God (Rom. 8.29). Despite the major influence of

Neoplatonic ideas on the immaterial and immortal human soul, it was from the beginning of his career that Augustine reflected on the presuppositions for a bodily resurrection after death and in the eschatological context.

Complex philosophical themes, such as time and eternity, found their way towards homiletic practice in the idea of the *totus Christus.* The wholeness of the eschatological Christ became a model for the perfection of all human persons in the resurrection. For Augustine it was a major issue that the body was to be included in this process of healing and perfection. In his early period from baptism until his ordination as a bishop, Augustine expressed a preoccupation with a repeated exegesis of the book of Genesis. The background of this reflection on the human body was coloured by his polemic with Manichean and gnostic groups. It was in the setting of the Donatist and Pelagian controversies that Pauline exegesis sparked Augustine's reflection on the human body in the resurrection. These considerations were leading in the selection of texts I have made to treat this topic. I have chosen for a text from the closing XXIInd book of *The City of God (De Civitate De*i XXII.14-17) on the bodily resurrection. As mentioned, further on in this book, I will examine this text again in the context of Trenton Merricks' physicalist anthropology. In *The City of God,* Augustine speculated in many details on the bodily resurrection of Christ. This reflection includes aspects of the bodily resurrection of all humans. Perfection, maturity and healing are keywords for Augustine's modus operandi envisioning the bodily resurrection in the closing of *The City of God (CG).*

> All are to have, in the resurrection, the mature bodies they had, or would have had, in the maturity of their manhood. However, it would really make no difference to have, in form, a child's or an old man's body, since there is to be no weakness of soul nor even any infirmity in body. (*CG* XXII.16)

Although Augustine's concern in Christology was to safeguard unity between the divine persons, he also emphasized the embodied character of the person of Jesus. Augustine even extended this notion of embodiment towards resurrection. For Trenton Merricks not dualism but physicalism has sufficient philosophical potency to stipulate that becoming embodied is necessary for becoming human. The consequence for Merricks is that, in his view, physicalism can account for God the Son having the body of Jesus and no other. In Trenton Merricks' opinion, each human person is a physical object, though being a human organism is not sufficient to be human.

Nonetheless, in Christian doctrine, Christ is not only bodily human but had also a sensorial human mental life. Augustine's discourse on anti-Apolliniarism in the context of Nicene theology found its result in his Christology. It was for this reason that Augustine highlighted that Christ must become fully human in order to be able to redeem humanity.

It is in this tension between physicalism and dualism that I plan to discuss the bodily resurrection. Yet, philosophical dualism faces the criticism not to evaluate the human body as an identity which constitutes the human person. Since Augustine showed special interest in the human body, I envisage him as a relevant partner in dialogue with religious studies and CSR.

1.2.4 What has been discussed? What's next?

An introduction is what it is: it is a starter and taster. Major topics and texts have been introduced, but many details remained unexplored. It is in the next chapters that I expect to be able to explore more in depth the interplay of the components of Augustine's careful discussion of place and function of the human body. At that point, the moment has come to introduce contemporary debate on the person of Christ from philosophical theology. From this confrontation, the topics that emerged from the readings of Augustine will guide reflection and dialogue on contemporary anthropology. Relevant topics include the concept of omnipotence, unity, theodicy, incarnation, the Christian God and the resurrected body.

As I have pointed out, Augustine's view on the human body was in its many facets closely related to his investigations regarding the humanity of Christ. The latter was a major argument to decide for a reading of Augustine's texts on Christology with the help of the trifold perspective: kenotic, *Logos-Sarx* Christology and eschatology. They correspond to the *impetus* of salvation which is the theological context of Augustine's Christology. God takes a human body in Christ and renounces from his omnipotence in the self-emptying act of the service of a slave in human embodied shape. The divine Word is the transcendent fundament for God's salvific presence in creation and in Jesus as a human person. Flesh and matter thus no longer signify an absence of God. They refer to a bond of love and unity: Augustine's *totus Christus*. In the perspective of resurrection, Augustine emphasized the embodied character. He did not hesitate to explore in detail the features and age of this perfected eschatological body.

In what follows, the aim is to read Augustine. Thus, in the next chapter, I will ask attention for a presentation of Augustinian texts. They have been introduced briefly in this introduction already, but they deserve more study in depth. Contrary to modern historical norms in theology, Augustine felt free to explain the story of creation in Genesis in the perspective of John's Gospel's theology of light and incarnation. This component of 'propelling theology' balances the self-emptying descendant *impetus* of the kenotic Christology. It facilitated Augustine's integration of Platonic and Neoplatonic concepts in his rationale. The latter underpinned his exegesis of Genesis and Paul. The same balanced theological approach can be found in his considerations on the celestial city in *The City of God*. These more in-depth readings of Augustine prepare the argument of this book for reflections on aspects of the resurrected Christ and humanity that may be relevant for future reflections on physicalism and resurrection.

Before starting this dialogue, it is necessary to extract some relevant insights from philosophical theology. The latter will be the subject matter of Chapter 3: 'Philosophical theology and the Body: Creation and incarnation'. The course of the argument will be directed by a personal motivated selection from contemporary debate on Christ in philosophical theology. These understandings enable to initiate a provisional experiment in dialogue as philosophical theology in Chapter 4: 'Christology in dialogue: Augustine and philosophical theology on the human body'. In this chapter, I discuss Augustine's texts on kenosis, divine Word and flesh and resurrection in the context of the work of Ilkka Pyysiäinen and Armin Geertz from CSR.

2

Augustine on the unity of Christ

Kenosis, Logos and resurrection

2.1 Augustine on unity: A ship that has sailed?

Reading Augustine questions theological concepts. Reading Augustine provokes old and new discussion on grace, providence and free will. Reading Augustine steers attention to the person of Christ. Even when Augustine discussed the most relevant topics in correlation with the giant Christ, it is impossible to label Augustine's Christology apart from anthropological debates in the body. He had found its most elementary articulations in texts of the council of Nicaea. In retrospect, he anticipated Chalcedon.

Finding the appropriate concepts to describe unity within the person of Jesus Christ was a major challenge on this council. Unity pertains to (divine) mind as well as to the body. Despite the distance over time, I look ahead to discuss some samples of early Christian polemics in dialogue with new speech on unity and the human body in philosophical theology and the cognitive sciences. Though, a dialogue takes identity and self-knowledge for granted. In the previous chapter, partakers in conversation have been introduced briefly. Now, it is the moment to explain aspects of Augustine's anthropology more in detail.

Augustine's reception of Nicaean texts has been studied widely. These books have enriched the current patristic debate on anthropology and Christology (i.e. Brian Daley, *God Visible*). Obviously, the scope of this book does not permit an exhausting exploration of the threefold motives: kenosis, *Logos-Sarx* Christology and resurrection. Hence, it is the aim of this book to read fragments from Augustine's written work motivated by questions from relative modern branches of scholarship. Thus, it is my intention to talk over aspects of Augustine's theory on mind and body in conversation with the present-day debate on anthropology. These theories include a variety of dualisms. However, physicalist theories on reality and the nature of the human person dominate. A first superficial glance at Augustine's texts may give the impression that he was a dualist. Then again, an anachronistic separation between 'rational' philosophy and 'fideist' theology is not appropriate for reading Augustine. The reception of his texts demonstrated the inheritance of a body–mind conflict. A growing dichotomy between philosophy and theology in the modern era arose. I hope that Augustine's unitarian anthropology eventually may inspire renewed debate on mind and brain. Biology and neuropsychology may offer relevant new insights from life sciences. Thus, a primordial response to Armin Geertz invitation to theologians can be made while reading Augustine in the twenty-first century.

In the selection of texts from the *corpus Augustinianum*, I preferred those that permit to illustrate fundamental aspects of Augustine's reflections on the unity of Christ. As mentioned before, not scholarly urgency but personal motivation related to pastoral practicalities was the reason for the choice. Thus, it is not the aim of this book to present detailed probes of concordance research. Instead, the threefold theological motifs – kenosis, *Logos-Sarx* Christology and resurrection – will take the lead in reading Augustine. Thus, I aim to direct the argument of this book in Chapter 3 to a discussion on topics on the person of Christ from philosophical theology. The works by Marilyn McCord Adams, Thomas Morris, Stephen T. Davis and Trenton Merricks are the partners in dialogue.

The first section is focussed on kenosis. It refers to universal topics such as suffering and death. An unexpected outbreak of a new virus confronts with the incongruity between the simplicity of structure in viral biology and the complexity of global concatenations. Hence, actual tendencies towards division and injustice ask for attention. Production processes have been spread over the world. Technology makes humans powerful. It makes them also vulnerable to inequality. In the second section of this chapter, the theological concept of *Logos-Sarx* Christology is in the centre. Augustine's path of humility in incarnation did prevent a collective debate in what became a body–mind conflict. He inspired René Descartes with arguments on the nature of the self. These days, in the light of renewed attention for embodied religion his path of humility may be relevant once again. The third section of this chapter reads a fragment of Augustine's *The City of God*. It centres on the concept of resurrection. Thus, the ever-returning question whether human life is dominated by chance or operates within a (common?) goal will be our lead. Darwinian terminology in popular debate survives as the fittest. Perhaps it is now the moment to try another dialogue.

Augustinian texts have been written by one author. However, traces of thinking a lifetime can be uncovered in fragments from his oeuvre. The texts chosen for this chapter cover a wide range of Augustine's life. Hence, changes and developments in Augustine's discourse may be noticed sideways. Obviously, for the tale of this book, it may be too complicated to trace details on correlations between texts and circumstances. These have been studied manifold in patristic publications. Thus, the reading of Augustine's texts will have its limitations and imperfections. Nevertheless, it is my aim to try to include this experiment in dialogue in philosophical theology, for the worse or for the better.

Firstly, I will explain the perspective of kenosis in Augustine's theology with texts from Augustine's *On Genesis against the Manicheans* and *On Trinity* (AD 388/390 resp. AD 400–28). Despite distance in time, these fragments share Augustine's exegesis of Paul's hymn (Phil. 2.5-11). In the assessment of humiliation and glorification of Christ, these books complement each other. They represent two different angles of Augustine's anthropology. In the second section on Logos Christology, Augustine's ambiguous reception of Platonic anthropology is our main point of attention (*Conf* VII). While impressed by Platonic anthropology of the immaterial soul, Augustine expressed his concerns for a defective understanding of humanity. Neglect of incarnation and the missing name of Christ were reasons to blame them for disregarding embodied humanity. This example of one-sided anthropology inevitably overestimated human intellectual capacities. In the third section, I draw attention to Augustine's final book, XXII, of *The City of God*. In this text, it will become clear that the human body will rise in close relationship to former bodily existence. This part of *The City of God* was written around AD 422–7. It reflects an apologetical perspective on the human body. Accordingly, the leading motive of the city of Jerusalem urged him to reflect on the perfected human body.

2.1.1 Augustine on kenosis: Why was this topic relevant for Augustine?

The viewpoint of a self-emptying God endorsed Augustine in his aim to explain the paradox between God's divinity and embodied humanity. This conundrum is an old one. In his rhetorical education, Augustine was confronted with a multitude of ideas on deities. Yet, Neoplatonism incited him to criticize deities for anthropomorphism. In reading the *libri platonicorum*, Augustine became convinced of God's immaterial nature (*Conf* VII.9.13). Repeatedly he rejected the current Stoic materialistic ideas on cosmology. However, elements of their theories on sense perception on emotions entered Augustine's anthropology. Cicero's influence in the work of Augustine was most prominent. Then again, Seneca also effected Augustine's writings. At first glance, this may appear contradicting. Yet, recent scholarship has demonstrated that Augustine's style of writing was far more than simply eclectic. He aimed for a personal synthesis from both Platonic and Stoic sources. Recently, both Sarah Catherine Byers and Charles Brittain published on Stoic aspects of Augustine's discourse.

Yet, this personal synthesis made it necessary for Augustine to give an explanation in his written and homiletic work for the embodied existence of the person Jesus Christ. Patristic theology stressed Jesus' simultaneous divine and human nature. Hence, ongoing reflection was necessary. Neoplatonic works postulated concepts of an ascending intellectual *impetus* towards divinity. Moreover, Augustine was in need to apprehend God's descending movement in incarnation. It started within creation. Though, the apex was to be found in embodied shape in Jesus. Thus, both creation and the birth of God in humanity asked for an explanation on contradicting divine presence, on the one hand, and human weakness, on the other hand. Yet, effective actions of mercy and corporeal healings were told in the gospels. They endowed Augustine with narrative for his sermons. Along this track, Paul's theological meditations on bodily redemption directed him towards a theology of kenosis.

At the pulpit, there were many occasions to explain this topic more in detail. In this section, I will bring up two major incentives that urged Augustine to be involved with kenotic Christology. A first topic is his former relationship with Manichean groups. They criticized the account of creation within the book of Genesis. Most of these Manichean groups valuated ascetism highly. Augustine criticized them for elitism. Consequently, Augustine propagated compatibility of bodily existence with divine salvation. The complex personality of Jesus Christ was his model. The efforts made by Augustine for a literal understanding of Genesis were in sharp contrast with extended Manichean mythology.

Augustine's metaphysical priority was the realm of divinity. Consequently, Andrea Nightingale branded Augustine's anthropology as transhuman. Nevertheless, it will become manifest in the subsequent readings that, in chronology, he chose for the primacy of the sensible realm. Principally, his concerns were signs and sounds. Hence, most probably, it was for pedagogical reasons that Augustine started his incentives within the domain of the sensible signs. No theology without narrative. For this reason, he needed an account which facilitated a discussion on relationships between time and eternity. Kenosis within Nicaean context of unity solved this problem for him.

A second topic that requires reflection is to be found in anti-Arian roots of Augustine's theology of Trinity. Neoplatonism offered models for Trinitarian structures. They were to a certain measure compatible with biblical testimony. Augustine faced the challenge to account for Christ's humanity. Thus, divine presence became effective in kenosis, as well as in theology of the Word.

This said, I will ask some time in the next paragraphs for texts from respectively *On Genesis against the Manicheans* and *On Trinity*. They reproduce Augustine's two angles in kenotic perspective. Both texts reflect different phases of Augustine's biography. The first text addresses the topic of creation, and the second Augustine's reaction to Arianism.

2.1.2 *On Genesis against the Manicheans*: Paradise lost or God's adaptation?

When newly baptized as a Christian, as a former member *(auditor)* of the Manicheans, Augustine felt the need to repudiate their rejection of the first book of the Bible. Augustine's method was simple. In a first commentary, he explained in what was recognized as literal sense the first three chapters of Genesis. Augustine ended his first book in an exposition on the seven days of creation. Each day was related to a phase in world history. In a second book, Augustine left his plan for literal exegesis. Instead, he chose the Jahwist part of Genesis (Gen. 2.4–3.24). Now, he focussed on figurative exegesis. As a skilled pedagogue, Augustine returned to a historical perspective further in the book. Thus, he transformed his discourse from literal exegesis to a prophetical perspective (*GM* II.24.37–27.41).

The text which now is going to be discussed is preceded by allegorical exegesis. The Cherubim and the flaming sword near the Tree of Life in paradise from Gen. 3.24 refer in a figurative style to temporal punishments and pains. However, these tribulations were not evaluated as negative. Additionally, Augustine made a positive connotation in their purifying function. Thus, Augustine completed his sketch of the human track towards the Tree of Life hopefully. Perseverance in temporal troubles (purification) will not destruct meaning in a context of fullness of love.

The fragment that asks for attention now focusses on the perspectives of history and prophecy. This methodological turn is a fine specimen of Augustine's variation in points of view. The verse, 'For this reason a man shall leave father and mother and stick to his wife; and they shall be two in one flesh' (Gen. 2.24), served Augustine's methodological aims very well. It was his ambition to link historical exegesis (Adam) up with prophetic explanations on Christ.

Some preliminary words on Augustine's theological stance are at this point appropriate. Rooted in Nicene Christology already in an early phase of his life, Ambrose may have provoked his sensibility towards unity within Trinity. In the next fragment, a tense relationship between the human and divine Christ was explained in a balance of kenotic and *Logos-Sarx* Christology. Quoting Phil. 2.7, Augustine commented on Genesis's account on offspring that separates from parents into a union of love for another human person. Thus, Augustine spelled out the process of purification in terms of perception of the embodied Jesus as the Word.

> But I promised that in this book I would consider first the account of things that have happened, which I think has now been unfolded, and go on to consider what they prophesy; and this still remains to be considered briefly, I don't reckon, you see, that this will take us very long once we have set up a kind of close signpost which will direct us through everything else. The apostle, you see, says that there is a great sacrament in the text which says: *For this reason a man shall leave father and mother and stick to his wife; and they shall be two in one flesh* (Gen. 2:24). He explains what he means by adding: *But I mean in Christ and in the Church* (Eph. 5:31-32). So then, what as a matter of history was fulfilled in Adam, as a matter of prophecy signifies Christ, who left his father when he said: *I came out from the Father and have come into this world* (Jn. 16:28). He didn't leave the Father spatially, because God is not contained in a space, not by turning away from him in sin, in the way apostates leave God; but appearing among human beings as a man, when *the Word was made flesh and dwelt among us* (Jn. 1:14). This again doesn't signify any change in the nature of God, but the taking on of the nature of a lower, that is, of a human, person. That is also the force of the statement, *he emptied himself* (Phil. 2:7), because he did not show himself to us in honor and rank he enjoys with the Father but cosseted our weakness while we did not yet have hearts and minds clean enough to see the Word as the Word of God with God. So, what else do we mean by saying he left the Father, but that he forbore to appear to us as he is in the Father? (*GM* II.24.37, transl. Edmund Hill)

Augustine's criticism was directed against boasted knowledge of good and evil (gnosis). Thus, he compared their pride with Adamic arrogance. Manichees' negative assessment of the domain of the sensible provoked Augustine's response: preference for pedagogy by example, particularly from the material world. In the sight of

Neoplatonism, Augustine's stance towards *sensibilia* may appear as contradictory. Then again, this approach permitted Augustine to bring together a reflection on the literal sense of Genesis' account of creation. Unity within the Son as a person in the Holy Trinity was preserved along these lines.

This said, three comments are to be made on the fragment of *On Genesis against the Manicheans:*

First and foremost, Augustine linked the text from Genesis he is about to explain to the topic of Christ and the Church as a sacrament. Paul's addition of Christ and the Church (Eph. 5.31-33) opened his perspective. In the account of children who leave their parents to find renewed union in marriage, Augustine included time, and, for that reason, imperfection. This insight has pastoral relevance. Augustine thus permitted brokenness and imperfect human love to participate in a marital bond between Christ and the Church.

> For this reason, a man shall leave his father and mother and be joined to his wife, and the two shall become one flesh. This is a great mystery, and I mean in reference to Christ and the Church; however, let each one of you love his wife as himself, and let the wife see that she respects her husband. (*GM* II.24.37)

Augustine's exegesis of Genesis in the context of Paul increased the impact of his message. He included temporality in God's self-emptying act in incarnation. Conjugal marriage love became a metaphor for incarnation. Despite his reputation for an ascetic ideal of marriage, Augustine stipulated that incarnated love did not neglect the human body. It includes human suffering and death within a universal perspective on salvation.

Then, secondly, this fragment reveals Augustine's prominent sensibility for unity between the three divine persons within the Holy Trinity. In handbooks, Augustine's Nicene orientation regularly has been coined as anticipating Chalcedonic (Western) Christology. In detail, those contentions may have been exaggerated. Though, on many topics, Augustine was in an intermediate position in the permanent discussion between the East and West. His reception and development of *imago Dei*- theory are exemplary. In the reception of Neoplatonic thought, Augustine was indebted to Origen and Ambrose (Gerald Boersma). As formula's stressed unity within the divine Trinity, the same strict perspective of unity was maintained by Augustine between the embodied Jesus and the divine Son.

Thirdly, as a last point, Augustine's kenotic Christology operated within the setting of God's adaptation on human weakness: *congruentia*. The Father 'cosseted our weakness while we did not yet have hearts and minds clean enough to see the Word as the Word of God with God. So, what else do we mean by saying he left the Father, but that he *forbore* to appear to us as he is in the Father?' (*GM* II.24.37) In the word 'forbore', Augustine underscored God's withholding action in kenosis. Thus, inclusion of horror and death within salvation history is a consequence. In this manner, restraint and mercy come forward as attributes of the Augustinian concept of God. These divine features are very helpful in a world forced to live in division, restraint and quarantine!

Why return in these days to the reading of Augustine's reply to Manichees and Arians? We have more in common than what separates us. Their bewilderments on the human body reveal it as a source of vulnerability. Recent problems with a pandemic disaster have demonstrated that even highly sophisticated societies are vulnerable. Even life-saving medical technology cannot answer the 'why' questions that raise in vulnerable groups that have been hit disproportionally by the virus outbreak. In this case, and in many others, the notion of perfection is ambiguous. Early Christian orthodoxy taught that it was not underneath God's worthiness to reside in imperfection. Struggles currently with uncertainty, suffering and illnesses probably benefit from Augustine's radical enclosure of negative aspects of life in healing and grace. These insights may have relevance in expressions of compassion and social coherence that emerge, even in the face of division and political conflict on the financial consequences of a virus outbreak. Inspired by these pastoral practicalities, I will briefly address three issues that may characterize pastoral significance of Augustine's kenotic stance.

Augustine's inclusion of the domain of (embodied) interhuman love may be valuable as a systematic device in the discipline of theology. In pastoral praxis, it offers consolation. However, it never should function as an excuse not to break the silence in power abuse and violence. Justice is the companion and foundation of mercy. Accepted brokenness never loses sight of the social dimensions of human love. The gift of inclusion involves a further task: compassion.

A second topic that came out is Augustine's well-balanced search for unity within the Holy Trinity. Augustine's subtle equilibrium between Platonist idealism and anti-Manichean sensualism still maintains a high standard for contemporary embodied study of religion. Physicalist, monist and dualistic varieties arose. In cognitive studies of religion, naturalistic methodology dominated. As a result, narrative remains in the shadow of second-order knowledge. Patristics' reflection on the narrative on the concept of unity may add relevant insights for the embodied study of CSR. Patristic texts reflect the slow rhythm of human responses on changes in religions. Patristic theology meditates on these rhythms.

A last issue to mention is Augustine's use of the *congruentia* concept. It is a metaphor for God's adaptation towards human limited capacities. The metaphor of God's restraint in kenosis is a vigorous example of merciful judgement in speech and act. This must be inspiring for recent debates on leadership in worldwide reaction on the effects of the viral outbreak. Prudence and restraint literally save lives. A less noble side of limited human expressions of *congruentia* can be noticed in examples of politicians' mercantilism these days. Augustine's considerations on society were indebted to antique notions of virtuous moderation and self-knowledge. Along these lines, he widened the notion of restraint supported by biblical narrative. We will return to the discussion of absence and constraint in Chapter 4 as major characteristics of Ilkka Pyysiäinen's suggestions to avoid a homuncular concept of God. For Augustine, a self-emptying God made humans more human.

2.1.3 *On Trinity*: Unity and mediation of wounded love?

Theophanies and God's omnipotence are core business in *On Trinity*'s second book. It is preceded by a first book which elaborates on equality between the three divine persons. In this phase of his life (AD 400–12), Augustine had found his point of departure in Nicene Trinitarian theology. This was not new. Yet, a comparison between Augustine's early Trinitarian theology – Monica's exclamation at the end of *On the good Life* – and *On Trinity* discloses Augustine's progression in biblical expertise. Arian debate had not ended with the declaration of a credal formula. Augustine's incentive was a discussion on the divine mission of the Son by the Father. However, theophanies happen in time and place. Theophany's narrative hides and discloses. More often, God's presence was manifested in signs and miracles. Can God remain totally divine while active in space and matter? This question rephrases the enigma of God's total divinity. It is in this framework of hiding and disclosure that the hymn on God's self-emptying action was phrased in Augustine's argument on Trinity.

Paul's hymn from the letter to the Philippians was quoted only a few times literally in this fragment. Yet, it resonates as a reference text. Literal quotation of Phil. 2.6 (Since he was in the form of God, he thought it no robbery to be equal with God) can be found in *On Trinity* II.1.3. Previous passages deliberate on the question whether the Son should be regarded as lesser than the Father in the form of a slave. On the one side, there was Arianism. Advocates exaggerated the Father's divinity. Therefore, unity within the person of Christ became problematic for them. On the other side, Augustine addressed gnostic and Manichean groups. These authors shared a negative judgement on creation and incarnation. Before I introduce Augustine's kenotic Christology within his theology of the Holy Trinity, I will briefly address the topic of Arianism.

2.1.4 Arianism

Even though Arianism regularly has been allied to the person of Arius (*c.* AD 250–*c.* 336), its influence reached much further. It is generally acknowledged now that the notion of Arianism has become a container concept. All theories from Arianism shared a tendency to make a disjunction between Christ's divine nature as a Logos and the human person Jesus. The latter was born from Mary's humanity. Initially, Arian debate had found its inducement in a concern for God's transcendence. God's creative activity involved transcendence within time and matter. Arius selected the verbs 'produced' and 'begotten' to describe the Son's emission from the Father. 'A perfect creature of God.' Thus, a historical Jesus was, despite his perfection as a creature, created by God's will. Salvation and reconciliation were his mission. His operation concentrated on wounded humanity.

To understand the scriptural narrative on Jesus within the context of the strict monotheistic religion of Israel was Arius' principal concern. Consequently, he downgraded the historical Jesus in metaphysics. It permitted him to affirm the absolute divine existence of the Logos-Son before the creation of time and matter. Ironically, even though unity was Arius' main concern, his account of Jesus as a creature threatened unity, since he propagated ontological division between the human Jesus and the divine Logos. For this reason, his ideas may be stamped as 'kenoticism *in extremis*'. The embodied Christ was a super-creature, because he was a mediator of creation and salvation. Along these lines, Arius explained that Jesus was begotten for all time by God to produce and order matter. Thus, he aimed to spell out how a transcendent Creator may create in matter and time without being touched by time and matter.

It is all too well known how these discussions in the council of Nicaea ended up: disputes on words. While Nicaea preferred to describe substance of the person Jesus as *homoousios* (of the same substance), Arian fractions chose for *homoiousios* (similar substance). It was the most important concern for participating bishops to confirm the Son's divinity in all aspects and in all times. The *ousia* concept defined unity. It was confirmed and refined at the council of Chalcedon (AD 451). Then again, in its reception in the East, its definition of unity was blamed for failure in description of Christ's mediation. Unfortunately, subsequent polemic contributed to schism between the East and West in the early church.

Augustine's approach to the debate on Christ's humanity stands out for its well-balanced quotation from Phil. 2.6 in the framework of Johannine theology. Verses such as 'I and the Father are one' (Jn 10.30) and the prologue of John's Gospel were among Augustine's favourites. In the second book of *On Trinity*, Augustine anticipated fictive opponents. He portrayed them as people who prefer to emphasize Christ's ontological inferiority to the Father. They opposed Augustine in quotations, such as 'The Father is greater than I' (Jn 14.28). Subordinationism thus was defended with Jn 5.19: 'Neither can the Son do anything of himself except what he sees from the Father doing.' In his reply, Augustine fortified his position, when he argued that scriptural texts demonstrate that 'the Son is no less than the Father, but that one is from the other' (*Trin* II.1.3).

Now that we have discussed some aspects of Augustine's idea on unity in Trinitarian theology, the moment is there to let Augustine speak himself. In this paragraph from *On Trinity*, he elaborated extensively on human action of Jesus Christ and on the unity between the divine personalities. These explanations served his anti-gnostic agenda. Despite many differences, gnostic groups shared a strong inclination to deny unity between actions of Jesus and the divine Logos. A fine specimen of Augustine's pedagogical preference for embodied aspects of Christ can be found in *On Trinity* II.5.8:

> For this reason, then, if both the Son and the Holy Spirit are sent thither where they were, we must inquire, how that sending, whether of the Son or of the Holy Spirit, is to be understood; for of the Father alone, we nowhere read that He is sent. Now, of the Son, the apostle writes thus: 'But when the fullness of the time was come, God sent forth His Son, made of a woman, made under the law, to redeem them that were under the law.' 'He sent,' he says, 'His Son, made of a woman.' And by this term, woman, what Catholic does not know that he did not wish to signify the privation of virginity; but, according to a Hebraism, the difference of sex? When, therefore, he says, 'God sent His Son, made of a woman,' he sufficiently shows that the Son was 'sent' in this very way, in that He was 'made of a woman.' Therefore, in that He was born of God, He was in the world; but in that He was born of Mary, He was sent and came into the world.

In this passage, Augustine conveyed his thoughts on the complex topic of a simultaneous mission of the Son in human shape, and his relationships in the setting of the Holy Trinity. His arguments with fictive opponents on the issue of the mission were settled earlier in this text. Now, he can spell out human action and speech of Jesus. He opted for a kenotic model of Christology. A consequence of this position is that a positive evaluation of immanent presence of Christ became distinguishing for Augustine's style of reasoning. Phrases such as 'but in that He was born of Mary, He was sent and came into the world' underlined a human origen of the saviour Christ' (*Trin* II.5.8). Nevertheless, Augustine did not indulge in immanentism. It was his contention to explain that the Son 'came into his own' (Jn 1.1). Along these lines, Augustine's view on redemption unavoidably extended to the realm of embodied religious life. Scriptural substance was offered in Gal. 4.4: 'When the fullness of time had come God sent his Son, made of woman, made under law, to redeem those who were under law.'

Three observations are to be made at this point. In the first place, Augustine's balance between immanentism and idealism is exemplary. These days, many people struggle with the problem of evil in combination with a concept of a transcendent perfect (homuncular) God. Augustine's extension of Trinitarian goodness towards day-to-day life in God 'who was sent into his own' does not solve problems from outside. It works in interiority. Contemporary debate on theodicy has focussed on divine attributes such as omnipotence. In response, kenotic theology flourished. In philosophical theology, a theory of two minds in Jesus clarified the debate on Jesus' anthropology. However, these theories probably lead to social Trinitarianism. Hence, a threat of tritheism looms. Accordingly, it may be noticed that Augustine's well-balanced teleological perspective is relevant in a search for sound theology of providence in the face of human suffering and death.

Secondly, a quality of Augustine's anthropology of unity becomes apparent in his account of unity in action between the Father and the Son in creation (*Trin* II.1.3). In this section, Augustine outlined the condition of the human Christ in a metaphor of a self-emptying God. Obviously, this was not new. However, in this passage he utilized the reductio ad absurdum figure. Exaggerated exegesis of Johannine theology (Neither can the Son do anything of himself except what he sees the Father doing, Jn 5.19) would according to Augustine imply

> that the Father must have walked on the water, or opened the eyes with clay and spittle of some other one born blind, and have done the other things which the Son appearing in the flesh did among men, before the Son did them; in order that He might be able to do those things, who said that the Son was not able to do anything of Himself, except what He hath seen the Father do. (*Trin* II.1.3)

Accordingly, Augustine shared early Christian criticism of anthropomorphism. Theology of the councils had focussed on the nature of the Son. Yet, as mentioned earlier in this chapter, this discussion on the person of Jesus was closely linked up to a steady debate on creation and the book of Genesis. Neoplatonism offered him the concepts necessary to harmonize two different accounts of creation in the book of Genesis. A theory of simultaneous creation solved the problem. The process of creation found its incentive 'in the beginning'. Though, it carries on overtime. Time stretches out towards perfection in the eschaton. Thus, Augustine aimed to give a fair treatment of both a cosmological account of creation in days as mentioned in Gen. 1.1–2.4a, and a second, anthropocentric, account of creation (Gen. 2.4b-25). The idea of a simultaneous creation made Augustine heading to the conclusion that creation happened 'in the beginning' but extended over time and years.

A third observation regards God's adaptation with respect to limited capabilities of humankind: *congruentia*. On the one hand, Augustine emphasized God's absolute transcendence. On the other hand, he underlined Christ's full humanity. In order to do justice to both polarities, he explained the relation between a divine Father and human vulnerability in terms of grace and providence. Once again, Paul's theological narrative was valuable for Augustine. The letter to the Galatians alluded to both characteristics of the risen Lord: perfection in the end and weakened condition of humankind. 'But when the fullness of the time was come, God sent forth His Son, made of a woman, made under the law, to redeem them that were under the law' (Gal. 4.4). Plainly, Augustine described God's salvific action as a synergy between divinity and wounded humanity. Hence, a vulnerable condition is simultaneously a highly valued state. A similar ambiguity echo's in Augustine's clarifications on the origen of humankind as 'made of a woman'. Augustine's explanation of the word 'woman' as 'the difference of sex' instead of 'privation of virginity' was in reaction to Arian Christology. 'Made of a woman' accordingly referred to Jesus' full humanity. Still, at the same time he emphasized divinity of the Word God's presence in the beginning. A fine-tuned balance in a theology of adaptation: *congruentia*.

Balance, criticism on anthropomorphic interpretation of miracles and a theology of adaptation characterize *On Trinity*. Obviously, in its genre, it is a theological treatise. Easily accessible metaphors are scarce. However, the aim for salvation is beyond time and matter. However, its incentives are given in temporal and material entities. In Augustine's theology, Christ is and will be the major sign in this process. In his embodied presence and sacramental state, he represents God's initiative towards humanity as a living sign. Augustine's rather positive view on the role of sensibilities in salvation was another reason to opt for kenotic theology. Thus, he legitimized the function of corporeal aspects in salvation. Hence, nature and time do not represent the ultimate purpose of humanity. Though, their support for education and *paideia* pertains to signs and the objects that teach and signify. They are direct at hand. They are the setting for human growth and salvation.

The model of a self-emptying God did not weaken God's power. It taught us to understand the human condition within the context of salvation. For Augustine, the theological devices were successful: balance, Nicene theology, humility, critical reception of anthropomorphism. They enabled speech on the mystery of divine presence in the world: as a mixture of good and evil. Kenosis is a theory of balance and of participation. In the next section, I return to the other side of Augustine's Christological balance: Christ the Word.

(a) Personal reflection

Every human person was born within an embodied context of human relationships. Yet, relationships reflect human love and joy. They mirror pain and brokenness in all kinds and gradations as well. Even a devastating global virus outbreak demonstrates our radical inclusion in the natural world. Being part of nature implies dependency in relationships, for better and for worse. However, human society persistently demands adaptation, socialization and formalization. Friendship and love are not exempt from the law of culture. Michel Foucault discovered discipline and power in social structures as backbones of relationships. However, the reading of Augustine leads me to discover that love and friendship may find empowerment in a theological concept of kenosis: restraint out of love.

Yet, these concepts of moderation show incompatibility with contemporary pluralism and liberty. However, hazards of disease and uncertainty reveal a crucial significance of empathy and flexibility in social relationships. Still, motives and motivations for empathy in relationships differ for individuals. Social distance and restraint in behaviour save health and overarches social divisions. We are all in this union: solidarity in benefits and adversaries.

An apparent desire for pluralism is in tension with longing for unity. Thus, these days we face a problem that shows common ground with Augustine's problem of unity in Jesus Christ. Augustine's well-balanced reflections on Platonic idealism as well as on anti-Manichean sensualism are exemplary. He underlined that God is not a humanly magician in miracles, and developed a theology of adaptation. Religion interprets phenomena and their interactions, and builds on the project of human identity. Discussion on identity easily deteriorates in a debate on 'who is in' and 'who is out'. Recent problems in climate change and health care demonstrate 'we are all in'. Patristic does study early Christian religious identity in a historical context. A special combination of divine attributes and human characters triggered me to read Augustine: the setting of present-day debate on the human mind and body.

2.2 Augustine on *Logos-Sarx* Christology: What was the relevance of this topic for Augustine?

Augustine's reception of Platonism has been studied over decades. Despite the many differences between these studies, there is one recurring theme: Augustine's ambiguity towards Neoplatonist anthropology. On the one hand, Augustine was eager to learn how to conceive a human soul as immaterial and eternal. Plotinus and Porphyry showed him the track. On the other hand, it was Augustine's wish to avoid their intellectual exclusiveness. Truth, as Augustine's imagination perceived it, should be accessible to all people. Their level of education or even (il)literacy may not hinder God's initiative for salvation. Neoplatonic theory evidently excluded uneducated people because of its complexity. For that reason, Augustine accused Neoplatonism of pride.

Meekness of Jesus was a leading example for Augustine. Christ represented humility as well as truth in the same process of incarnation. Hence, it may not be surprising that Augustine made every effort to achieve a balance in his Christology between a 'lower' kenotic perspective and a 'higher' *Logos-Sarx* theology.

In the first sections of this chapter, it was noticed that a kenotic perspective calls attention to embodied and temporal aspects of redemption. It is along these lines that Augustine calls in the topic of humility and incarnation. Hence, in what follows now, I will focus on mutual effects of the perspectives of kenosis and *Logos-Sarx*. In a paragraph from the seventh book of Augustine's *Confessions*, a kenotic stance merges with Johannine theology of the Word. In this manner Augustine conveyed the story of his reading from the *libri platonicorum*. He explained his confusion and talked about Paul's hymn from the letter to the Philippians. Hence, Christ's humility contrasted with puffed-up philosophical experts. They refused to recognize divine and eternal truth in Christ's humanity.

The seventh book of Augustine's *Confessions* tells a persistent story of Augustine's quest for truth. At the outset of this seventh book, he presented himself conceiving God as a material entity, dispersed in an unlimited space (*Conf* VII.1.1). Consequently, a material God is transient. This was unacceptable for Augustine (*Conf* VII.4.6). When astrologists were not able to explain cosmological order of providence (*Conf* VII.6.8-7.11), he finally read books of the Platonists. He compared their teachings with scriptural narrative (*Conf* VII.9.13-14).

The text on Augustine's encounter with Platonists is what calls our attention in the following paragraph. The fragment finds its continuation in a section in which Augustine told about his search for God in withdrawal from senses (*Conf* VII.10.16). However, the senses were of great importance for Augustine in pedagogy. Hence, in Augustine's opinion, all created things honour God in their participation in divine order (*Conf* VII.12.18–13.19). All created things inherit being from God. Consequently, they all communicate their relationship with God's goodness. This ontological friendship culminates for Augustine in the person of Jesus. He is a mediator between time and eternity. Accordingly, Augustine blamed Platonism not to mention incarnation. Hence, this seventh book finds its continuation in a pivotal book eight: the story of his conversion in the garden. It is preceded by exemplary stories of Victorinus' conversion (*Conf* VIII.2.3–4.6). In this context, Augustine's critical lecture of the *libri platonicorum* is a prelude to the central happening of the book: his confession of Christ as the centre of his future life. Thus, no message without criticism and precaution against the pride of Platonists. Augustine's major blame was their refusal to recognize Christ as a *doctor humilis*. A simplistic grumble against Platonists' disbelief? Time to have a closer look at Augustine's text.

2.2.1 *Confessions*: Pride and unity?

The first part of this fragment tells the story of Augustine's preliminary reasons for being proud. Yet, he was convinced that God used the vice of pride to motivate him for the cure of it. Thus, Johannine theology helped him to outline a theology of healing. However, he recognized the Platonic message as incomplete. It did not mention the world's refusal of the Logos coming in the world. The Word arrived on what already belonged to Himself: He came to his own.

> And Thou, willing first to show me how Thou resistest the proud, but givest grace unto the humble, and by how great an act of Thy mercy Thou hadst traced out to men the way of humility, in that Thy Word was made flesh, and dwelt among men: Thou procuredst for me, by means of one puffed up with most unnatural pride, certain books of the Platonists, translated from Greek into Latin. And therein I read, not indeed in the very words, but to the very same purpose, enforced by many and divers reasons, that In the beginning was the Word, and the Word was with God, and the Word was God: the Same was in the beginning with God: all things were made by Him, and without Him was nothing made: that which was made by Him is life, and the life was the light of men, and the light shineth in the darkness, and the darkness comprehended it not. And that the soul of man, though it bears witness to the light, yet itself is not that light; but the Word of God, being God, is that true light that lighteth every man that cometh into the world. And that He was in the world, and the world was made by Him, and the world knew Him not. But, that He came unto His own, and His own received Him not; but as many as received Him, to them gave He power to become the sons of God, as many

as believed in His name; this I read not there. (*Conf* VII.9.13, transl. Pusey).

Significantly, Augustine's account of Platonist Logos theology was balanced in the familiar hymn in Phil. 2.6-11. Augustine offered an authoritative biblical explanation for the missing part of the message in Platonism. Thus, he quoted Matthew's gospel on God's special revelation to the little ones. 'I thank you, Father, Lord of heaven and earth, because you have hidden these things from the wise and the intelligent and have revealed them to infants' (Mt. 11.25). Augustine attached a description of Christ's mission of humility for those who are laden and in search of rest (Mt. 11.28-29).

> Again, I read there, that God the Word was born not of flesh nor of blood, nor of the will of man, nor of the will of the flesh, but of God. But that the Word was made flesh, and dwelt among us, I read not there. For I traced in those books that it was many and divers ways said, that the Son was in the form of the Father, and thought it not robbery to be equal with God, for that naturally He was the Same Substance. But that He emptied Himself, taking the form of a servant, being made in the likeness of men, and found in fashion as a man, humbled Himself, and became obedient unto death, and that the death of the cross: wherefore God exalted Him from the dead, and gave Him a name above every name, that at the name of Jesus every knee should how, of things in heaven, and things in earth, and things under the earth; and that every tongue should confess that the Lord Jesus Christ is in the glory of God the Father; those books have not. For that before all times and above all times Thy Only-Begotten Son remaineth unchangeable, co-eternal with Thee, and that of His fulness souls receive, that they may be blessed; and that by participation of wisdom abiding in them, they are renewed, so as to be wise, is there. But that in due time He died for the ungodly; and that Thou sparedst not Thine Only Son, but deliveredst Him for us all, is not there. For Thou hiddest these things from the wise, and revealedst them to babes; that they that labour and are heavy laden might come unto Him, and He refresh them, because He is meek and lowly in heart; and the meek He directeth in judgment, and the gentle He teacheth His ways, beholding our lowliness and trouble, and forgiving all our

sins. But such as are lifted up in the lofty walk of some would-be sublimer learning, hear not Him, saying, Learn of Me, for I am meek and lowly in heart, and ye shall find rest to your souls. Although they knew God, yet they glorify Him not as God, nor are thankful, but wax vain in their thoughts; and their foolish heart is darkened; professing that they were wise, they became fools. (*Conf* VII.9.14, transl. Pusey).

A few observations are to be made now.

Firstly, as was observed previously in the fragment from *On Trinity*, in *Confessions,* Augustine declared his faith in the same well-balanced manner. Johannine theology on the advent of the Word was contextualized in the threefold structure of the One, Logos and Psyche. Hence, it seems, it is typical for Augustine that *Logos-Sarx* Christology found its theological balance in kenotic exegesis. The major part of Augustine's quotation from Paul was repeated literally. Still, some details from Augustine's quotation of Paul can offer some insight into the bishops' specific bias towards a kenotic perspective.

In the quote of Paul's hymn on Christ's descendance in the shape of a slave, Augustine added some extra words.

For I traced in those books that it was many and divers ways said, that the Son was in the form of the Father, and thought it not robbery to be equal with God, *for that naturally He was the Same Substance.* But that He emptied Himself, taking the form of a servant, being made in the likeness of men.

Augustine's Latin text reads: *indagavi quippe in illis litteris varie dictum et in multis modis, quod sit filius in forma patris non rapinam arbitratus esse aequalis deo, quia naturaliter id ipsum est: sed quia semet ipsum exinanivit formam servi accipiens, in similitudinem hominum factus.* Comparison with Paul's biblical text learns that Augustine added the words *quia naturaliter id ipsum est* (for that naturally He was the Same Substance).

Despite the differences between the literary genre of Augustine's *Confessions* and *On Trinity*, the addition of these words suggests an urge to stress unity *in nature* between the Son in shape of a slave and the Son in divine form of the Father. A relevant observation for discussion in the chapters that follow further in this book is

Augustine's presupposition to achieve perfect unity between absolute transcendence *and* existence as an embodied human person.

The concept of unity has been advocated in different varieties. Philosophers studying religion, such as Thomas Morris and Richard Swinburne, concluded along different lines that the hypothesis of a man who simultaneously is divine and human not necessarily contradicts logic and arguments. Both philosophers consequentially have turned their attention to Chalcedonian Christology. Personally, the step towards unity within a human person asks for the courage to step on an invisible road. I try to walk on this road. So far, I did not stagger alone.

Secondly, there is Augustine's observation of reading the *libri platonicorum* on theology of the Word. Though, he searched in vain for words on the glorification of the Word, Jesus, as the glory of the Father. At first glance, it appears to be a simple rebuke of Platonists not having reached the fullness of wisdom in Christian revelation. However, Augustine criticized Neoplatonic sources in the context of a discussion on pride and humility. In response to some gnostic groups, he disapproved of their tendency to estimate the Logos ontologically inferior to the One. Biblical narrative taught Augustine to conceive the glorification of the Word (Jesus) in eschatological perspective as unified perfection. Thus, ontological equality between divine persons supervened over differences between the divine persons in the Holy Trinity.

These observations clarify the concept of unity between God and humankind within the person of Christ. Modern theories on the human person sometimes tend to bias one of the aspects of humanity – soul or body. Problems arise when both must be taken into account. Augustine's theology exemplifies how holistic approaches can improve insight in both aspects of existence. Despite the reputation of a dualist, Augustine's meditations on the person of Christ direct towards a holistic concept of unity in anthropology.

Thirdly, in the aftermath of discussion on ontological equality between the Father and Son – Christ's humility – Augustine criticized philosophers' pride. This criticism had found strong biblical corroboration in quotations from the Gospel of Matthew (Mt. 11.25-30).

At that time Jesus declared, 'I thank thee, Father, Lord of heaven and earth, that thou hast hidden these things from the wise and understanding and revealed them to babes; yea, Father, for such was thy gracious will. All things have been delivered to me by my Father; and no one knows the Son except the Father, and no one knows the Father except the Son and any one to whom the Son chooses to reveal him. Come to me, all who labor and are heavy laden, and I will give you rest. Take my yoke upon you and learn from me; for I am gentle and lowly in heart, and you will find rest for your souls. For my yoke is easy, and my burden is light.' (RSVCE)

Moreover, Augustine quoted Paul's juxtaposition of the wise and fools on their refusal to praise God in the Word Jesus (Rom. 1.21-22). 'For though they knew God, they did not honour him as God or give thanks to him, but they became futile in their thinking, and their senseless minds were darkened. Claiming to be wise, they became fools' (RSVCE). Apart from his deep respect for Platonist wisdom, Augustine's criticism aimed at their preferred metaphor of vision. He reproached their blindness caused by pride.

I will return to Augustinian criticism on pride further on in this book, particularly in dialogue with the work of Thomas Morris and Ilkka Pyysiäinen. Augustine's plead for humility, or at least for moderation, offers a wise contribution to public debate on humanity's relationship to nature.

(a) Personal reflection

Unity is an ambiguous concept. The spell of fragmentation hovers over the desire for union, since humankind experiences nature in a virus outbreak. While connected on an invisible scale, this bond shatters the nexus of economy, social life and health. Stigmatizing and diverting dynamisms are apparent already in politics. On a smaller scale, people blame and struggle with each other for things that happened outside their power. On a global scale, solidarity threatens to be limited to borders of countries or to people of a select, elitist community. Simultaneously, splinters from human relationships in social and economic perspectives are subjected to centripetal forces. In the silence of a society in quarantine, sometimes individuals who normally do barely notice each other now take care of each other.

In Augustine's assessment, realms of existence – bodily and spiritual – are tightly connected. Temporality thus becomes immersed with eternity. In reading Augustine, I see a holistic perspective. It desires for integration of spheres of life, even in periods of health crisis. However, this may not happen without tensions. New conflicts rise, while old wounds still must heal. Reading Augustine, I see these tensions not to be resolved within the sphere of personal lives. Augustine taught to endure differences and tensions in an attitude of humility. Thus, modesty denotes submission to exterior circumstances. Humility demands a sense of community. The early Christian bishop Augustine learned to concentrate on things that happen within the sphere of our influence: self-knowledge.

More than once in my life, I had to resign to the exterior circumstances. Is this Stoic fate? Is it an expression of divine Providence? Augustine's theology of the Word clarified divine presence within time. He identified human life – and its limitations – within a universal order. Without fatalism, humility offers a track to cope. It helps to realize that divine presence – or submission to cosmic providence, or even chance – can help to accept what happens. The face of modesty within the person of Christ helped me to focus on unity. Unity hovers over the world, despite fragmentation and conflict.

2.3 Augustine on resurrection: Why was this topic relevant for Augustine?

Augustine's anti-Manichean polemics had left traces in his assessment of the human body. Yet, in a greater part of cases, he started his account with a reference to an example or a scriptural passage that mentioned sensible observations. At first sight, this appears to contradict Augustine's preference for eternity and interiority. However, I think this chronology served his pedagogical purposes. Yet, in the twenty-second book of *The City of God*, Augustine elaborately reflected on embodiment and eschatology.

He had found scriptural foundation for these considerations in Paul's letter to the Rom 8.29. 'For those whom he foreknew he also predestined to be conformed to the image of his Son, in order that he might be the first-born among many brethren' (RSVCE). Thus, in his considerations of bodily eschatology, his involvement within a debate on grace and predestination resonated. Augustine's quote from Paul's letter to the Romans found its personal address in the verse before: 'We know that in everything God works for good with those who love him, who are called according to his purpose' (Rom. 8.28). Details on embodied resurrection thus were framed within the community of God-lovers. And, from this group, the promise is that those who have been called according to this purpose will be reformed according to the image of the Son. From a twenty-first-century perspective, the procedure of vocation makes an elitist impression. Hence, in the next chapters, I will discuss Augustine's ideas on bodily resurrection in juxtaposition with physicalist statements on bodily resurrection.

For Augustine, the concept of the *totus Christus* was authoritative. Its capability to transform transcendent initiative into material reality became wrapped up in a web of interhuman relationships. It made Augustine bear in mind that the Church manifests itself as a mixed community. Thus, the bishop of Hippo considered that the Church is a reality within time, and extends over past towards eschatological future. His preference for embodied reality within pedagogical situations served a doctrinal as well as a pastoral aim. Along these lines, doctrine turned out to be inclusive of the entireness of creation. Hence, pastoral practicalities found their expression in homiletic work: the preaching bishop.

The twenty-second book of *The City of God* is dominated by its rhetorical aim: a conclusion. Its main subject matter is the beatific vision. The community of the saved thus will enjoy this vision. It is of principal significance. The risen human person in soulish-embodied state is the most important example of God's miracle in creation. It includes bodily reality. It ends in beautiful perfection. Despite positive reflections on what happens in restoration of bodily defects in resurrection, Augustine chose to end his deliberations in an apophatic tone. Hence, he concluded that human reflections are not capable to imagine divine reality, announced by miracles (signs!) accompanying the apostles' work. Negative views on the human body thus found critical response in Augustine's inference on immortality. Not by nature, but because of God's decision (*CG* XXII.26).

Augustine's exclusion of the *massa damnata* from the happy end goes against contemporary common sense on equal rights and justice. Expectations and demands on human development regularly find their foundation in the laws of physics and life sciences. These disciplines pertain to universal laws and principles. However, research in cognitive sciences revealed once more a unique importance of education and social factors, such as entrance to health care and jobs. In the crisis in global health, many vulnerable groups have demonstrated being victims of inequality: poor access to health, resources and political influence. In Augustine's ideal order of society, justice reigns and love perfects. For now, it is a consolation to see how this hopeful reality included bodily existence, even in its brokenness. Even in a period of horrors, hope becomes sensible at hand for a fragmented society. A kenotic perspective!

2.3.1 *The City of God*: Perfection in unity?

Augustine's willingness to put his ideas on bodily resurrection in words found its basis in *imago Dei*-theology. Particularly in his later work, Neoplatonic theory underwent revision and was transformed within a vivid discussion on grace and providence. In *The City of God*, Augustine mentioned the concept of conformity *(similitudo)*. It became the foundation of a relationship between the individual risen body and the image of God:

> The text of St. Paul which speaks of the 'saints predestined to become conformed to the image of his Son' is susceptible of two interpretations. It may refer to the purely interior man, as does the parallel text: 'And be not conformed to this world but be transformed in the newness of your mind.' For we are certainly 'conformed' to the Son of God when we are 'transformed' so as not to be 'conformed to this world'. A second interpretation is that we are to be 'conformed' to Him in immortality, as He was conformed to us in our mortality. And, in this sense, the test refers to the resurrection of our bodies. However, we must remember that, even in this interpretation, the 'conformity' is no more a matter of the size of our bodies in the resurrection than the 'measure' in the other text refers to size. It is a matter of maturity. All are to have, in the resurrection, the mature bodies they had, or would have had, in the maturity of their manhood. However, it would really make no difference to have, in form, a child's or an old man's body, since there is to be no weakness

of soul nor even any infirmity in body. And so, if anyone cares to defend the position that we are to rise with the same shaped body we had at death, there is nothing to be gained by pursuing the debate. (CG XXII.16)

In this text, surprisingly, the concept of perfection is clarified in terms of realized maturity and growth. The measure to which potential adjustment towards perfection may happen surpasses human wisdom. It is part of divine insight. Accordingly, it reflects Augustine's apophatic perspective.

The text that precedes this fragment is significant for the apprehension of Augustine's discussion. A paragraph on bodily outcomes of measure and age within resurrection paves the way: humans do rise as persons aged thirty-three. They rise in a perfected body. Their bodies thus will be finished in harmony with their destination that was given in creation. Obviously, it was Augustine's aim to make the point that the process of creation finds its extension in the growth of bodies and souls. Yet again, the goal of unity within the human person determined the atmosphere in Augustine's discussion.

In the following section, Augustine elaborated on the enigma whether humans will rise in their bodily sexes. The latter position was confirmed. Augustine concluded that in an eschatological state, lust no longer dominates the differences between sexes. Genital organs thus function according to will.

In agreement with the scriptural narrative of a woman who was a widow of seven men, Augustine argued that marriage will not last in resurrection. Humans will not be married in heaven. They will be 'as the angels'. Augustine hastened to comment: risen humans live in 'immortality and beatitude, not like them [the angels MC] in being spirits without bodies, nor like them in the resurrection, since angels had no need of a resurrection, simply because they could not die' (CG XXII.17).

This remarkably detailed account of humans in resurrection gives reason for three further observations. Firstly, Augustine's concept of eschatological perfection is unmistakably embodied. Though, Augustine harmonized contradictory principles of transcendency within perfection in his text. Its completion is expressed in bodily presence: healing from infirmities and the promise of perfect measure. Yet, Augustine's apophatic move at the end of the fragment restored balance in his argument. In the end, appropriation of divine knowledge to the measure of healing and growth led Augustine to the conclusion that potential measure already has been given from the beginning of creation.

Secondly, in his conclusion that humans do rise in a body aged thirty-three, it is the aim of Augustine to include the human perfected person in his argument for unity. Hence, he included the domain of the senses in resurrection. Along these lines, completion within the order of time found final resolution within the number thirty-three: the age of the crucified and risen Christ. In this fashion, Augustine incorporated human suffering and disability within perfection. God's presence in signs and sacraments had a crucial role in a process of transformation: limited humans will be conformed to the image of God.

These days, identity over natural death is a topic of intense debate in philosophy. A body-snatcher model and the falling-elevator of Peter van Inwagen assist philosophers in tentative theories on death. I return to the topic of death in the next chapter. A confrontation of these theories with dualism, ascribed to Augustine, is in danger to incite anachronistic errors. Despite this caution, it is promising to read Augustine's account on resurrection in dialogue with contemporary questions on identity.

Lastly, Augustine's concept of perfection in resurrection was coined as angelic. In *On the Happy Life*, the concept of *vita beata* was discussed in the context of the virtue of moderation. Dominantly, Augustine focussed on the practicalities of a virtuous life. Scenes of the dialogue were staged with objects and affairs from day-to-day life. Despite his pragmatic orientation, Augustine's position on the happy life exemplified his opinion that *vita beata* cannot be reached on earth. Though, a maximum of happiness can be found for those 'who possess a merciful God' (*HL* II.21).

(a) Personal reflection

Bodily diseases may cause horrible sufferings. In the face of pain, disordering consequences of accidents, war and poverty, Augustine's expressed firm confidence in the thesis that each human person, in whatever condition, reflects the image of God. This may be naïve in the face of the pandemic. However, Augustine's efforts to include all aspects of human embodied reality in providence and grace postulated sources of consolation and hope. Thus, Augustine inclined his ears to the words of Paul: 'We are to be "conformed" to Him in immortality, as He was conformed to us in our mortality'. In this view, exchange between extremes of bodily, political horror and divine healing are actual and factual. Its effect is now. However, who will be able to trust these words when humans experience vulnerability? Who will be able to find comfort in the moments that external circumstances threaten the course of life?

The step to have confidence in providence lifts actual phenomena of suffering and uncertainty to a new level of absolute interdependency. More than once, I have experienced being dependent. In pastoral practice I often see people struggling with the painful loss of autonomy. However, at the other side of existential threat, miracles can be seen. Despite Augustine's astute reputation in his theory of grace, the aspect of mercy referred not exclusively to doctrinal aspects of salvation. Augustine's theology of grace included actual communal life, even in incompleteness and disharmony. In his ecclesiology, he never aimed for a small elitist church. Even in face of evil effects, Christ transforms into *se ipsum*. It gave my life a foundation. However, it asks for daily courage to step on the invisible bridge. Thus, no fatal lapse until yet.

2.4 What has been discussed? What's next?

In this chapter, we have followed a threefold movement: kenosis, *Logos-Sarx* Christology and resurrection. This has led us from descendance in incarnation (kenosis) towards unity within the person of Christ in *Logos-Sarx* Christology. In the last section, we have finished in eschatological perfection with a fragment from *The City of God* on bodily resurrection. This tripartite drive has exposed three attributes of Augustine's preoccupation with the topic of unity.

The kenotic approach has disclosed insights on the person of Jesus Christ over time and eternity. During His life, he was recognized by Augustine as effectively present as a divine and human personality. Even though to a limited extent, we have studied two texts from different periods of Augustine's life. To a limited measure, they enable a comparison of Augustine's stance towards anthropology in these different periods. In his early commentary of the book of Genesis, the focus was on his discussion of Gen. 2.24. 'For this reason a man shall leave father and mother and stick to his wife; and they shall be two in one flesh.' The image of conjugal marriage functioned as a metaphor for incarnation. Incarnation in this self-emptying context did not imply that God had left aside aspects of divine existence while incarnated. Hence, God does not exist spatially but immaterially. Embodiment did not limit divine capacities. I will ask renewed attention to that specific issue in discussion with Marilyn McCord Adams in the next chapter.

Even in an early stage of his theological career, Augustine showed himself as loyal disciple of Nicene theology. Yet, unitarian Trinitarian theology did not hold him back from the principle of adaptation: *congruentia*. God adjusts saving action to limited capacities of wounded humanity. In Augustine's argument, mercy did not imply God losing whatever aspect of his divine essence while being close to humanity. In the following chapter, I will return to this topic in a discussion with Thomas Morris' two-mind theory.

Despite the distance over time, Augustine's discourse on humans who leave their parents in order to live in union with other humans still has relevance for pastoral praxis. It qualifies the domain of (incomplete) love for the fullness of divine saving action. Yet, without reduction of moral responsibility in determinism.

A second text from *On Trinity* focussed on aspects of Augustine's later reflections on unity. It revealed a balance between immanentism and idealism. Especially this phenomenon offered reasons for systematic theologians to discuss Augustine's theology of Trinity in the context of Chalcedonian Christology. More than once, this functioned as a justification for the conclusion that Augustinian Christology was not extremely renovating. Nevertheless, Augustine's description of unity in action between the Father and the Son underlines the concept of unity within the whole Son. It is in this context, in the next chapter, that I will come back to recent theories of social Trinity and monism.

Unity was not restricted to the existence of Jesus as a person. Augustine's theology extended Jesus' activity to effects in daily existence. Consequentially, incarnation includes the impact of divine presence within the realm of senses. The latter is closely related to

Augustine's track of humility within corporeality. Since it was his aim to unite salvific action with temporality, the principle of *congruentia* enabled Augustine to conceive of theological complexes such as the *totus Christus*. In homiletic work, the bishop of Hippo explained this theology of salvation on many occasions in the metaphor of *Christus medicus*. Hence, particularly Augustine's theology of mediation is a promising area for rich discussion with embodied theories in CSR.

The second text we have seen was from Augustine's *Confessions*. From the fragment that was studied, it became evident that Augustine's synthesis of kenotic and Johannine theology of the Word has its place in the centre of his reception of the *libri platonicorum*. In his annotations on these books, Augustine expressed admiration as well as criticism. Admiration, because these texts permitted him to reflect on God's immaterial existence, and consequently, on a human immaterial soul. Platonist's pride and their omission of Christ's name and of the story of his glorification were his major points of criticism. Yet, he praised their wisdom for recognizing the Word within the divine Logos. Pride made them blind. In the end, they missed insight into Christ's humility and meekness.

Augustine's account on the *libri platonicorum* in *Confessions* was included in a discourse on providence and the discovery of the name of Christ. Many times, he explained how details of his biography gave him guidance in the context of divine wisdom: Christ. It gave him the opportunity to think on transcendent *and* embodied reality. Providence and theodicy still provoke philosophers. In response, they developed theories on determinism and ethical reflections. Marilyn McCord's Christology of horrors was an attempt to see how Christology can face death in its sad consequences. In the closing chapter of this book, I will return to Augustine's approach of Platonists in discussion with Ilkka Pyysiäinen's concept of God in relationship with absence and constraint.

Lastly, Augustine's view on resurrection was at stake. At the end of *The City of God*, eschatological perfection and bodily resurrection were studied. His synthesis of embodiment and eternal existence makes this fragment, despite its speculative character, significant for debate on life after death. We have seen that his idea on human bodily resurrection is modelled after Christ's resurrection at the age of thirty-three. Along these lines, scriptural narrative on the risen Lord made it possible for him to include human disability in eschatological perfection. Thus, human bodily resurrection will be of angelic nature, but not without body. Angelic features of resurrection will find completion in a perfect measure that will be actualized in the risen state. Every human person received her measure within creation. Still, knowledge of this measure is included in divine knowledge. It surpasses human knowledge. The question whether perfect happy life may be accessible within time or merely after this life still divides opinions. A perfection given 'in the beginning'.

The threefold movement kenosis, *Logos-Sarx* Christology, which finally has ended in resurrection, will also direct the lead in the next chapter. However, patristic texts no longer are the main course. Instead, the focus will be directed on contemporary Christology. Philosophical instruments of analysis and elements of theological doctrine do not evidently cooperate smoothly. Hence, a format for dialogue is required.

In a self-emptying projection on Christian doctrine, debate on divine omnipotence and limited capacities of the historical person Jesus asks for attention. Marilyn McCord Adams will lead the argument in an assessment of kenotic Christology. Furthermore, the relationship between the divine Christ and the human servant will be evaluated with the help of the publication of Stephen T. Davis, *Encountering Jesus*. His earlier book, *Logic and the Nature of God,* explained incarnation in kenotic perspective. As a contrast, we will take some time for Thomas Morris' *The Logic of God Incarnate*. He studied Jesus the Word of God and his human existence.

A third and last perspective in the next chapter is the resurrection and the body of Christ. While discussing consequences of a theory on bodily resurrection, Trenton Merricks' article 'Split Brains and the Godhead' will inspire our reading of the fragment of Augustine's closing book of *The City of God*.

In the last chapter, Augustine's insights that have emerged from the first three chapters of this book lead to a discussion with the work of embodied theories from CSR scholars Armin Geertz and Ilkka Pyysiäinen. Thus, I will argue that, despite methodological disparities, the challenge for an (imperfect) dialogue between the disciplines is urgent and necessary.

3

Philosophical theology and the body

Creation and incarnation

3.1 Was Augustine doing philosophical theology?

Until yet, we have seen samples of Augustine's thought that disclose aspects of his view on the human body. Now, the time has come to make a further step exploring the bishop's texts in the context of philosophical theology. As a coined discipline it is relatively recent. However, its debates were relevant in Augustine's age, as they are in our days. Thus, arguments from logic operate in a debate on theological presuppositions. Though, in the last decades doctrinal topics such as Trinity, incarnation, creation, anthropology and Christology have attracted renewed attention in philosophy of religion. In the subsequent sections, I return to Augustine's perspectives on kenosis, classical *Logos-Sarx* theology and resurrection. This recurrent threefold perspective on Augustinian texts is meant to be discussed with the assistance of contrasting views from recent philosophical theology. However, it will become clear that, despite the differences in methodology and perspectives, contemporary debate on Christology still discusses topics from Augustine's era.

In philosophy of religion, it has been noted that a majority of world's population is participating in some form of religious praxis or belief. Thus, great names from science and cultural domains addressed the phenomenon of religion: for example, Albert Schweitzer, Martin Buber, Emmanuel Levinas, Bertrand Russel and Ludwig Wittgenstein. They represent a variety of views. Though, no philosopher can disregard their contributions to intellectual heritage, including their views on religion. Further, recently relevant issues such as the nature of evil, human's capability for knowledge, consciousness and reality urged for renewed attention to the phenomenon of religion. A widened scope of cultural sciences for non-Western scholarship revealed that a division between philosophy and theology is not evident in worldwide traditions of wisdom.

Hence, many scholarly activities on the nature and meaning of religion have been encouraged: theological epistemology, ethics of belief, religion and science. Philosophical theology partially was shaped by evidentialist discussion. Evidentialism propagated that trust in belief ought to be justified by proportional quality of evidence. Consequently, philosophers such as Richard Swinburne *(The Christian God)* and John Schellenberg *(Divine Hiddenness and Human Reason)* participated in this renewed perspective on religion. Yet, evidentialism was refined to reliabilism. According to this revised theory, confidence in religion can be justified in proportion to the reliability of its means of justification, with or without consciousness of the believer. Reformed philosophers defended the thesis of an innate sense for divinity, the *sensus divinitatis*. Thus, a discussion on the question whether this special sense warrants the truth of God's existence emerged (Alvin Plantinga, Nicolas Wolterstorff). More and intense debate in philosophical theology focussed on Christ's personality and his place within the Trinity. In the subsequent sections of this chapter, a distinct picture emerges that shows that kenotic theories had strong effects in theology. However, they were criticized for their social concepts of Trinity (Thomas Morris, Trenton Merricks).

Criticism on Christians' confidence in resurrection, incarnation and creation was expressed in early Christianity by works of Celsus, Marcus Aurelius, Porphyry, and gnostic opponents. In Chapter 2, some of these arguments against Christian accounts on creation have been mentioned. Apologetics always was an ingredient of conservative Christian groups' rhetoric. Similarly, it can be found in circles of fundamentalist Islamic and Buddhistic groups. Yet, also without intention to proselytize, a keen academic interest in the question 'to what extent religion can participate in a dialogue between humanities and physical sciences has incited a renewed interest in evolution and religion. Within the discipline of philosophical theology, debate focussed on topics such as existence of God, divine attributes (omnipotence, omniscience, goodness) and pluralism.

From the prospect of philosophy of religion, Augustine was a realist. He scored relatively low on the scale of scepticism. Yet, an early dialogue such as *Against the Academics* demonstrates Augustine's dependence on sceptic dialectics, as well as his rejection. Still, his confidence in a transcendent intellectual reality is obvious. Reason was deferred by original sin. Yet, even in weakened state humans are made capable to participate in eternity and transcendence. Evil had no ontological status. Augustine captured it in a theory of deficiency of goodness. Yet, in almost every sermon Augustine struggled with the topic of suffering and evil sin. Christ was not only present in cosmic shape but also active within daily life. Hence, sacraments of the Church functioned within the sphere of time.

Words were of a special kind in Augustine's cosmos. As signs they were arranged as instruments for communication, even on divine matters. Augustine's theory of language balanced on both *via positiva* (scriptural exegesis *De doctrina Christiana*, defence of orthodox doctrine) and *via negativa* (apophatic accents in theological discourse, e.g. *Trin* XV). Atonement thus was attached to the concept of grace: God's supervenient activity within time. Augustine's concept of creation was not limited to the moment 'in the beginning'. His theory of extended creation over time joined his reflections on the world's beginning with perfection in the end. In his explorations on divine interaction with humanity and creation, the personage of Christ was a unique model.

Cognitive Science of Religion studied cognitive functions in relation to the development and praxis of religions. Not only rituals, religious practice, sacred spaces but also bodily aspects of religion have contributed to the understanding of religion in a wider setting of cognitive sciences: psychology, sociology and neurosciences. In its initial phase, it was seldom that scholars from CSR and theologians cooperated in research projects. However, in the work of Armin Geertz more collaboration between history of religion, evolution and cognitive sciences has been contended for. Hence, in this perspective the observations from the second chapter on Augustine's pedagogical chronological preference for religious activity within the domain of the senses (sacraments, scripture) is suited to be discussed later in this chapter. I have chosen topics that have triggered my attention in both pastoral and scholarly work: suffering, humility and resurrection, and they will lead the discussion. Hence, it is a personal perspective. Consequentially, I do not claim to be complete, or even meticulous in the readings of Augustine's texts that follow in this chapter.

In biology, attention for study of religion came up not only in neurosciences but also in evolutionary biology. Interdisciplinary study of religion in biology and theology showed itself productive in the study of religious experience. Social function in the development of *Homo sapiens* made religion acceptable for those who focussed in research on ethical effects of religion. Even though it is biophysical reality that constitutes brains' involvement in religion in this type of research, theology has revealed its potential to incite debate in environmental discussions. These days society faces new challenges that require pliability in personal and social life. Augustine's special eye for the position of humankind in creation and the concept of self-knowledge is still instructive.

Neurosciences have a reputation for highly specialistic research in a complex laboratory environment. Yet, among many other phenomena, religion has attracted attention. Since some decades, collaboration between scholars within the discipline of CSR has produced many new insights. Neurologist Lawrence Barsalou clarified the central role of embodiment in the growth and transmission of religion, especially in visions, rituals and belief (Barsalou 2005). Armin Geertz asserted that research on the development of the human brain in the context of emerging culture may open new routes in theology: a synergy between evolution, history of religion and cognitive sciences (Geertz 2010).

In this approach, religion is studied as a particularly cultural phenomenon. Though, the emergence of religion from a natural process cannot give ultimate answers for the question whether God exists (Visala 2014b, 56–73). However, in my perception this perspective not necessarily excludes input from patristic theology. Patristic texts usually were written with the assumption that God exists and that writing about God makes sense. For this reason, in Chapter 4, it is my aim to plan an experiment in dialogue between

Augustine on the concept of God in the context of Armin Geertz and Ilkka Pyysiäinen.

Patristic authors often assumed God's existence, but varied in their answers on God's nature and presence. So did Augustine. However, he was not blind for scepticism and the force of their argument. As original sin had weakened human's abilities to acquire knowledge, in Augustine's view, grace was God's response on humanity's powerlessness. These concepts were explicated in doctrine and scriptural testimonials. Put side by side with authors such as Sextus Empiricus or Cicero, Augustine's philosophical scope was explicit theist and biblical in nature. Though, paralleled with the work of Tertullian, Augustine was more permissive for insights from Hellenistic and sceptic philosophy. Augustine's reason was disturbed, but not completely disabled.

3.2 How was Augustine received in philosophical theology?

From the perspective of theology, Augustine's doctrine on the Trinity frequently was received as unitarian. In the perception of his criticists, Augustine's emphasis on unity between the divine persons withheld him from a full-fletched articulation of attributes of the separate divine persons and their relationships. In philosophical theology Augustine's Trinitarian model was assessed as a psychological model.

Philosophical theology in early Christianity cannot easily be described. Divisions between philosophy and theology were perceived from a different angle. Early Christian theology thus emerged within a variety of philosophical theories in metaphysics and ethics. While Augustine criticized philosopher's pride, it was Cicero's exhortation to wisdom that made him ready for reflection on topics such as evil, happiness, providence and self-knowledge. Augustine's works sometimes expressed apologetical arguments. However, in most of the cases Augustine's work discussed theology to explore Bible in a pastoral setting. Theory of emotion was postulated by Stoic authors and adapted by Augustine to his own purposes. So was his theory of perception, reformed by Platonic readings. Anthropology remained work in progress throughout Augustine's life.

Among patristic authors, Augustine emerged as a theologian of the will. Therefore, not surprisingly, recent philosophical theology quoted Augustine in debates on atonement and providence. Thus, Alvin Plantinga and Nicolas Wolterstorff (reformed tradition of philosophical theology) have been influencing theology of grace. Nevertheless, the reception of Augustine's thought on evil was much criticized. Marilyn McCord Adams blamed Augustine for conditional benevolence (Adams 2006, 29–32).

From the perspective of literary genre, Augustine's dialogues ask for special attention. Augustine remodelled specimens from Cicero and Plato. The topics discussed were taken from current debates in philosophy: providence, self-knowledge, evil, happiness, human soul and its capacity to know and feel. From the style of reasoning, he aimed for a personal synthesis that was not in contradiction with basic Christian doctrine of Trinity. Yet, at some points Augustine made more in-depth analyses on issues already discussed in the dialogues. He returned to the topic in *On Trinity*.

Christ's mediation, and the terminology for the reflection on this topic, had dominated theological debate as a heritage of the Arian controversies in the decades before Augustine. In response, theologians sought suitable concepts that enabled them to reflect on urgent doctrinal matters. Credal formulas and council documents always echo contemporary debates in philosophy and politics. Hence, dispute on dualistic anthropology and Christology inspired Origen to explore Hellenistic thought in the context of the Bible. God's transcendence in the Word became a vehicle in theology. It secured a refined relationship between divine oneness and division over time. In the aftermath of Origen's writings, many misunderstandings on the origen and destiny of the human soul *(apokatastasis)* followed in monastic circles. Debate on icons and post-Chalcedonian argument on philosophical reliability of Trinitarian terminology led to a division between the East and West in the Church.

Attacks from the dualist side generally aimed at doctrine of creation and incarnation. More than once, Augustine was blamed for anthropomorphisms by former Manichees. In the East, Cappadocian theologians centred on the concept of transformation in Christology and developed a social concept of Trinity. As a result, disputes on the two wills that operated within Christ in a unified action asked for attention.

Similar disputes have a continuation in contemporary philosophical debate. In a naturalistic setting, scholars have employed empirical data from lobotomy patients in conjunction with psychiatric research on multiple personality disorders. Their aim was to find models that enable analogy: two types of consciousness simultaneously operating within one person. Criticists have contended that, when overstretching this analogy (Christ), unity is in danger. Divine persons thus represent merely manifestations of one and the same goodness. Yet, modalism leaves no place for persons. Incarnation involves existential participation of divinity in time (creation) and in Christ. Modalism potentially excludes human existence from divinity. Along these lines, Christ would have been a 'modus' of divinity within humanity, and therefore not fully human. The reality of salvation is in danger.

Social Trinitarianism as described by Cappadocian fathers characterized persons of the Trinity as members of a family. This type of Trinitarian theology assessed the persons and their mutual relationships in detail. Shared attributes of divine persons are omnipotence, omniscience, goodness and moral perfection. A bond of mutual love connects the Three in One. Opponents contended that this branch of Trinitarianism easily advances towards tritheism. Otherwise, Nicene credal formulas were resolute on their claim for divine essence of the Three Persons. Early Christian texts regularly explicated atonement in terms of victory in Christ's resurrection. His death paid ransom for humanity bound in evil. Thus, humanity's victory of horror and death is effectuated in triumph. Despite Augustine's extensive written oeuvre, it is significant that it was mainly Boethius' influence that incited debate on dialectic in theological doctrine. Thus, medieval monasteries and schools copied numbers of Boethius' translations of Aristotle: the *logica minor*. Boethius' definition of a human person as an *animal rationale* was standing out as a firm basis.

While a fair part of ancient philosophy was accessible in Latin translations, another major impulse came from Scotus Eriugena (AD 810–77) with his translation of pseudo-Dionysius. The reception of Augustine's work stimulated a theology of vision and grace in affirmative modus *(via positiva)*. By contrast, Eriugena's synthesis proposed the *via negativa*. His work on providence and his book *On the Division of Nature* were both condemned by Church. A further division between theological doctrine and philosophical reflection was in the making.

Anselm of Canterbury (AD 1033–1109) was repeatedly characterized for his transitionary position. A strong argumentative style in his texts revealed a new tendency in theological reasoning. Most famous were his texts on the existence of God: that which surpasses our conception of the most excellent proves the existence of God in our minds and in the cosmos. Anselmus' dialectical style was new and personal. In a later stage, Petrus Abelardus (AD 1079–1142) further refined the theory of language. While major parts of Aristotle's texts were not yet accessible to him, he was unique in his view on signs. Later, he would be coined as nominalist.

When logic became more and more the area of specialized scholars, theology and philosophy became gradually further separated. Translations from texts on dialectics were read at universities of Paris, Bologna and Cologne. As a reaction, scholastic methods of argumentative theology were developed. Thomas Aquinas, Bonaventure and Duns Scotus were talented masters in this method. They had, on their turn, stimulated a further extension of this method in the thirteenth and fourteenth centuries.

By then, religious orders had become major determining factors in the respective styles of theology. With their great names, growth of a further division between philosophy and theology speeded up. Thomas Aquinas (AD 1224/25–74) profited from Aristotelian terminology in his works. Though, at that moment, it was not long ago (AD 1215–31), that Church leaders protested against reading of Aristotle's metaphysics and natural science at the universities of Paris and of Toulouse. Theology was rooted firmly in revelatory sources: scripture and divine authority. That was the *momentum* for philosophical theology: it was on track towards theological argument with the help of instruments from dialectics and philosophy.

At the end of the nineteenth century until the first half of the twentieth century, neo-Scholasticism emerged in Roman Catholic theology. In part, this was a reaction to the increasing attention for the *via negativa* (Hume, Kant, Bultmann). Modern criticism on the human being's capability for (biblical) knowledge were sometimes perceived as sceptical by doctrinal *magisterium*. Thus, a revival of optimism on the successful combination of human reason and divine revelation as defended by Thomas Aquinas became a yardstick for orthodoxy in popularized theology. Since then, a reaction to what was called onto-theology was raised by theologians who corroborated critical approaches to reason's capability understanding religion. Thus, not only Emmanuel Levinas but also Jean-Luc Marion engaged in theology speaking on what God is not, and on his absence.

From the perspective of philosophy, both logic-positivism and Wittgenstein's philosophy of language had a strong influence on twentieth-century theology. Their criticisms on theology incited encouraging reactions. These included phenomenological study of religion (logical positivism) and study of practicalities in religious language (prayer, performative ritual). Logical positivism challenged the content and meaning of religious claims. Since none of them can be verified or reproduced as in empirical science, the need for verifiability contributed to further division between philosophy and theology. In a later stage, empirical study of religion emerged in the format of sociology of religion and phenomenology of religion. During the most recent decades, this branch of study participated in a wider approach of comparative study of religions. In the twentieth century, Wittgenstein's approach to religion targeted his criticism on the traditional theory of meaning. He focussed on patterns and pragmatics of language and signs in religion. Accordingly, inductive methods were doing the work for Wittgenstein. He inspired investigations of theologians' speech on afterlife, prayer, evil, suffering and the existence of God.

Both, logical positivism and Ludwig Wittgenstein's linguistic turn have inspired reactions that incited new approaches to the study of religion: cognitive science of religions. As a discipline CSR studies religious praxis and phenomena in combination with insights from (empirical) cognition sciences. In consequence, aspects of Wittgenstein's insights on function of language in religious behaviour (performative speech) can be examined in combination with embodied aspects of ritual and prayer. Though, philosophical theology, as it is known in our days, concentrates mostly on presuppositions of doctrinal topics such as Trinity or God's existence. Religious epistemology is a leading thread in this debate. CSR invites scholars to connect study of religions to the wider branch of life sciences. However, this opportunity involved also a risk of reduction.

Natural theology situates itself in-between these branches of study of religion. It does not limit its methodology to natural sciences. It includes insights from epistemology in its debate on natural religion. Consequentially, it is less focussed on empirical investigations. In its contemporary shape, a branch of natural theology explores arguments from Intelligent Design theories. Hence, sometimes this division of research functions in apologetical popular debate in conservative Christian circles. However, in its academic shape, it is driven by a posteriori arguments.

Philosophical theology over last decades is a mixed phenomenon. It discusses *a priori* arguments in combination with a posteriori arguments and their limitations. Among a multitude of differences, often there is a common point of departure in philosophical theology: Chalcedon's Christology. Some scholars have developed modern forms of Trinitarian doctrine. They produced a variety of deliberations on implications of aspects of Christian doctrine: creation, resurrection or identity in afterlife. Some of these authors were driven by apologetical concerns (e.g. evidentialist). Though, many of them had a keen interest in aspects of Christian doctrine and their philosophical implications. Physicalism, philosophy of consciousness, rethinking the evil: it all already happened long ago.

3.3 Does Augustine's kenosis meet the standards of a horror defeater?

The picture of Jesus as a friendly saviour flourishes not only in the pews of churches but also in popular belief and art. Even an angry Jesus attracted a wide audience in a 1995 Utrecht exhibition on the Angry Jesus *(Jezus is boos)*. A profile of Jesus who participates in existential joys and sufferings attracts the (negative) affection of larger groups of mixed types of believers and non-believers.

In kenotic theology, the mind of Jesus was discussed frequently. These theories assessed Jesus' divine and human capacities and their interaction in his historical body and senses. Recently, Thomas Morris tried to clarify this relationship with the help of analogies from psychiatric disorders. Though, in response to radical kenotic theology, already in nineteenth-century Oxford theology, attempts were made to develop theories on Jesus' perfection (presumption of perfection).

Characteristic qualities will be detected easier in contrast with dissimilar perspectives. Thus, it is the aim in the next sections to read Augustine in parallel with a distinct dissimilar vision in contemporary theology. In each section, I will select one topic to focus on. The motivation for this choice is subjective. These subjects have touched me in my readings of Augustine. At the end of each section, I will add some personal remarks in reaction to the respective stages of Marilyn McCord Adam's horror-defeat model.

In her Gifford Lectures and in *Christ and Horrors*, Marilyn McCord Adams argued for a three-stage model to face the threat of senseless suffering. Mainly, these phases lead to transformation of suffering. It is a model that makes the subject receptive for divine pedagogy within time and life. McCord Adams' message is that integration of secondary signs from interior divine order in the biography of the subject makes less vulnerable to loss of meaning. Despite McCord Adams' interest in compassion, she did not seek her support in social Trinity. On the contrary, she criticized kenotic models of Christology, and developed her own view on Trinity and salvation.

In the previous chapter, I discussed Augustine's proclivity to include imperfect love in his order of salvation. A quote from *On Genesis against the Manicheans* can help us to remind Augustine's attitude towards sub-optimal human love. However, he never lost sight of the ideal of divine perfection in face of horror and division. Augustine dedicated a multitude of words to the explanation of evil as non-being. While liberated from the problem of evil, it made him susceptible to criticism of one-sidedness and voluntarism. Still, a careful reading of his texts incites the emergence of a more subtle picture.

What about modern Christology and kenosis? Not an easy road! A firm tendency to acknowledge the permanent development of Jesus' own sense of divinity and divine origen of his thoughts and actions can be found in the contributions of Stephen T. Davis. His 'Jesus was Mad, Bad or God' argument made C. S. Lewis' contribution to Christology famous again. It was coined the MBG argument (Davis 2002). On the topic of the person of Jesus, Davis was convinced that Jesus over time became increasingly aware of his divine origen and consciousness in thought and action. Stephen Davis stuck to a Chalcedonian type of Christology: Jesus was believed to be truly human and truly divine. Debates in publications of Davis discussed the question whether Jesus Christ possessed essential divine properties during his earthly life. Hence, Jesus Christ's continuing contribution as Word and second person of divine Trinity, while embodied as a human person, raised questions on the process of eternal creation. At the same time, being divine and living in a human body in kenotic theories was explained as voluntarily abstinence from exercise of divine capacities. Nevertheless, Stephen Davis followed what was branded as a higher Christology. He concluded 'that Jesus Christ failed to have some divine properties but was still God, and had some divine properties but was still a human being, and he failed to have some human properties, but was still a human being and had some human properties, but was still God' (Davis 1983, 129).

Let us return now to Marilyn McCord Adams. Augustine was criticized for voluntarism by McCord Adams. In 'The Problem of Hell: A Problem of Evil for Christians', Adams appealed for a non-anthropocentric perspective of universal salvation (Adams 1993, 311–13). In this view, hell is a consequence of the problem of evil. Nevertheless, Marilyn McCord Adams rejected Augustine's idea of *massa damnata*. No less than universal salvation will be able to do justice to the huge amounts of individual suffering. In this viewpoint, justice correlates to divine love. Despite her critical stance towards Augustine, I see that McCord Adams shared common ground with Augustine's theology of grace, especially in its soteriological function and purpose.

In *Christ and Horrors*, Adams reviewed positive and negative features of 'free will approaches'. As a positive aspect, she praised consequential dignity of human life and body, on the one hand. On the other hand, McCord Adams referred to God's defective order of creation in state of paradise. Already in pre-lapse status, Adam and Eve were limited in the perception of consequences from their actions. They were inexperienced. They were embodied and not able to oversee what their actions were to incite (Adams 2006, 36). Since innocent people can become victims of actions, Adams discerned that moral categories fail to explain individual and common horrors. Non-optimal conditions of existence as well as relationships make individuals vulnerable. Thus, the condition of human embodiment was chosen by Adams to expound on existence within 'a material world of real or apparent scarcity such as this' (Adams 2006, 37). Non-optimal conditions of life determined to a large degree Adams' assessment of creation in metaphysical order. Suffering is a consequence of metaphysical mismatches in human nature: an ensouled bodily being that grows and develops during life.

A second mismatch is detected by McCord Adams between human nature and material world, particularly in necessities of life. Scarcity thus incites aggression. It provokes an attitude of 'survival of the fittest'. Lastly, McCord Adams observed a mismatch between a creating Godhead and humanity. The metaphysical gap between Creator and creation makes communication between human beings and God a risky endeavour. Thus, trust becomes costly. McCord Adams' preliminary way out is that metaphysical mismatches are 'in the first instance, a function of what things *are* and not of what anyone does' (Adams 2006, 38). A cosmological hypothesis, driven by loving assimilation and union, offered a lookout. Within creation, creatures are transformed. They assimilate to divinity. Yet, human creatures that are vulnerable to horrors that can take away life's positive meaning, are eventually able to participate in this saving process (Adams 2006, 39). Adams adhered to a Chalcedonian approach of Christology, which insists on God who had become human. In a reversed movement, incarnation opened human's access to God's unifying aims in creation. Human non-optimal existence thus participates in divine solidarity (Adams 2006, 108).

Until yet, I have focussed on dissimilarities between McCord Adams and Augustine. Despite this, she shared much with the bishop of Hippo. Firstly, her threefold cosmological thesis aims to describe the transformation of a subject in a process of transignification. Existential horrors are meant to be assimilated. Their goal is union within the order of being. Recently, in Augustinian scholarship, it was David Meconi who argued for Augustine's theory of deification (Meconi 2013). Despite the reception in theology of Augustine as a theologian of the will, Meconi argued that humanity's deification is the primary purpose of Christian salvation in Augustine's Christology (Meconi 2013, 234). Hence, Adams revealed in agreement with Meconi's perception of Augustine, a strong involvement in suffering and lack of meaning in the life of individuals. The same worry for the poor and sick can be noticed numerous times in Augustine's homiletic work. Though, from a theological perspective, Augustine focussed on Paul's absolute contingency of God's grace. Thus, he explained theology of grace along the lines of the Pauline metaphor of milk for the little ones (1 Cor. 3.2). McCord Adams insisted that the huge amount of individual human suffering only is justifiable within the universal order of salvation. It seems to me, that her picture of this order shows many parallels with the Augustinian order of grace.

But there is more. It is time now to return to the fragment from Augustine's *On Genesis against the Manicheans,* as discussed in 2.1.2. The text invokes God's presence in humankind's vocation for union in love. Love drives individuals who are linked within friendships. Augustine commented about two individuals who leave their parents in order to become united in love. Previously, I have suggested a reading of Augustine which includes fallible human love. An overarching perspective of the *totus Christus* facilitated him to incorporate suffering and deficiency. Hence, in this section, I will raise some points in which Augustine may be relevant for McCord Adams' *desideratum:* an organic relationship between a suffering person and God (stage I horror defeat).

As Augustine linked his comments on Genesis (Gen. 2.24) with Paul's Christological focus (Eph. 5.31-32), the argument shifted from literary (Adam and Eve) towards a prophetic perspective. Along these lines, Augustine's comments on marriage and human love operated as metaphors for incarnation. Prophetical exegesis incited Augustine to construct a metaphysical framework, which included human condition in its hope for (lost) perfection. Accordingly, sin and brokenness are consequences of the fall. In his sermons, Augustine never missed an opportunity to give explanation on human weakness in combination with God's multiform presence in Scripture and creation. Further, in this section I will raise the question whether Augustine was able to fulfil McCord Adams' wish for healing of meaning-making capacities of suffering persons (stage II horror defeat).

Another kenotic position asks for consideration. Augustine chose Paul's kenotic hymn on Christ from the letter to the Philippians, to focus on the Christological turn that was to be made in the change from historical towards prophetical perspective. Hence, he made an anthropocentric turn in exegesis. God's self-emptying presence within human suffering served Augustine's rhetorical purpose. Augustine's Christ is near people who must face horrors. Once more, a parallel between Augustine and McCord Adams' vision on recreation of our relationship with the material world (stage III horror defeat).

The relevance of Augustine's kenotic move resonated in his commentary on Genesis, particularly where the word 'sacrament' was underlined: Christ as a sacrament. Paul described union in life and household at the end of the fifth chapter of his letter to the

Ephesians. He quoted from the book of Genesis. His conclusion was that the bond of human love finds its foundation in love between Christ and the Church. 'For this reason, a man shall leave his father and mother and be joined to his wife, and the two shall become one flesh.' This is a great mystery, and I mean in reference to Christ and the Church; however, let each one of you love his wife as himself, and let the wife see that she respects her husband (Eph. 5.32-33, RSECV).

With the introduction of the Church, Augustine proposed time. The ultimate purpose of the Church was situated in a heavenly Jerusalem. Still, in chronology Augustine's focus was on the communities he served as a bishop. Previously, I made a similar observation regarding Augustine's view on unity and embodiment: senses first in chronology. In his sermons, but also in exegetical treatises such as *On Genesis against the Manicheans*, it becomes clear that Augustine was alert to non-optimal human condition and abilities. For this reason, the *Christus medicus* topic was one of his favourites in preaching. In his exegesis in *On Genesis against the Manicheans,* it is a sensible and fleshly union that becomes a sacrament of unity between Christ and the Church. Augustine echoes down-to-earth advice on interhuman love: 'However, let each one of you love his wife as himself, and let the wife see that she respects her husband.' It affirms his attention to mutual love and for (non-optimal) human existence in his theology. Thus, a revision of McCord Adams' statement that Augustine neglected this aspect in a voluntarist style of theology of evil is welcome. In more detail now is Marilyn McCord Adams' three-stage hypothesis on horror-defeating.

Stage I: establishing a relation of organic unity between the person's horror-participation and his/her intimate, personal and overall beatific relationship with God.

Stage II: healing and otherwise enabling the horror-participant's meaning-making capacities so that s/he can recognize and appropriate some of the positive significance laid down in stage I.

Stage III: recreating our relation to the material world so that we are no longer radically vulnerable to horrors.

Adams observed that this 'paints a portrait of the *ante mortem* state of Christ's human nature that looks quite different from the one perfectionist patristic and scholastic thinkers drew' (Adams 2006, 66). Our readings from Augustine's commentary on Genesis have pointed out that particularly the aspect of *congruentia* between God's saving initiative and human's weakness raises questions on McCord's criticism of Augustine.

Augustine's kenotic turn in his exegesis of Gen. 2.24 was centred on Phil. 2.7. Furthermore, Paul's hymn was quoted within the context of Johannine argument. Fulfilment of prophetical significance for Christ's human presence was underlined. It is particularly Jesus' sensible presence that makes Augustine's arguments effective. In self-emptying love of God, humanity's horrors participate in a universal process of cleansing: envisioning the Word of God. Christ's sacramental presence in non-optimal human love is thus accomplished over time. Augustine:

> So then, what as a matter of history was fulfilled in Adam, as a matter of prophecy signifies Christ, who left his father when he said: *I came out from the Father and have come into this world* (Jn. 16:28). He didn't leave the Father spatially, because God is not contained in a space, not by turning away from him in sin, in the way apostates leave God; but appearing among human beings as a man, when *the Word was made flesh and dwelt among us* (Jn. 1:14). This again doesn't signify any change in the nature of God, but the taking on of the nature of a lower, that is, of a human, person. That is also the force of the statement, *he emptied himself* (Phil. 2:7), because he did not show himself to us in honor and rank he enjoys with the Father but cosseted our weakness while we did not yet have hearts and minds clean enough to see the Word as the Word of God with God. So, what else do we mean by saying he left the Father, but that he forbore to appear to us as he is in the Father? (*GM* II.24.37, transl. Edmund Hill).

McCord Adams characterized miracles, healings, as well as Jesus' resurrection as 'all of these are down payments on and signal Divine power and intention to follow through with stage III horror defeat – with cosmic re-creation that will place us in a non-toxic relation to our material environment, one that will bring an end to the power of matter to ruin personal meaning' (Adams 2006, 72). In the context of this *desideratum,* a functional parallel with Augustine's fragment from *On Genesis against the Manicheans* II.24.37 emerges. McCord Adams' evaluation of sensible expressions from God's divine action in miracles and signs – down payments on Divine power that enable a non-toxic relationship with our environment – reveals functional similarity with Augustine's perspective on Christ as the Word that incarnated. Though, it did not diminish divine governance within Trinity. However, as it becomes evident later in the text, Augustine preferred a kenotic perspective.

Radical kenotic theories often require a social model of Trinity. In social models, God the Son is after his death restored to his original exalted state, under supremacy of the other two divine Persons. This is in contradiction with Chalcedonian Christology. Nicaea and Chalcedon stressed unity without mixture of divine and human natures. In response, radical kenotic theologians in the nineteenth century determined how a humanly Jesus diverted from his cosmic functions (Adams 2006, 90). Relative kenotic theology was launched as a reaction. In this model, a theory of two spheres was conceived within the person of Jesus. It was imagined how these could cooperate as systems of relationships. Although different, they were not sealed off from each other. As they were linked in Jesus' one will, it was possible for Christ to restrain from the exercise of some divine powers. Hence, Jesus was at some moments able to act within the limitations of human capacities.

At first glance, the model of cooperating spheres and their relationships contradict Augustine's efforts to explain Christ in unity within dual natures. Augustine's Christology is based on being *and* relationship. More than once, radical kenotic theologians lamented the influence of Hellenistic philosophy on early Christian theology. McCord Adams interpreted divine Being as personal. Though, she criticized theologians who prefer to let 'psychological and moral categories do the work that metaphysical notions were meant to do' (Adams 2006, 105).

Marilyn McCord Adams returned to metaphysics. She commented on Richard Swinburne's Christology in *The Christian God*. His model of social Trinity as a Three-souled God was scrutinized. Yet, Swinburne stated that divine plurality presumes cooperation, unified in perfect goodness and omniscience. Consequentially, from this perspective, the person of Christ is best conceived in a two-mind theory. These theories work with a hypothesis that the divine Word exercised out of its comprehensive consciousness a form of control over its narrower human consciousness. *Vice versa*, the human mind would have partial access to the content of the divine Mind. Yet, traditional Christology requires union within the person of Christ, in such a manner that the divine Word characterizes him. Therefore, ontological dependence cannot easily be described as a reflexive relation. Assumed nature differs from the divine Word. However, the Word cannot be distinct from itself. McCord Adams thus pleads for a tighter metaphysical connection between mind and body. Especially, the person of Jesus requires clarification. A tight metaphysical bond between mind and body makes Him more susceptible to participation in human horrors. Stage II horror-defeat requires God's initiative. It transforms synergy between human and divine action into expression of normative design. Augustine's theory of grace in a nutshell.

Despite many differences in method between McCord Adams' horror-defeating model, and Augustine's theology of evil, it may be noticed that McCord Adams' description of the interaction between humanly horror participants and divine initiative bears resemblance to the function of Augustine's inclusion of imperfection. *Congruentia* was clarified in the context of Pauline kenosis. Unity was a presupposition which was discussed by Augustine in his responses to Arianism in *On Trinity*. In his commentary on Genesis, theology of *congruentia* had its consequences: an anthropological turn. Probably, Augustine's theology of evil was voluntarist. Yet, this made him not blind to the horrors of the individual in situations of scarcity, to metaphysical mismatches, and disunion in non-optimal human existence. Thus, Augustine's kenotic theology did not coerce him to corroborate the social Trinity McCord Adams criticized.

Personal reflection

Marilyn McCord Adams established a relevant theory on horror defeat. Many people face injustice in suffering. Loss of meaning happens to the most vulnerable and makes them more susceptible. It happens to the most fortunate and can make them helpless. Thus, this model is highly relevant in pastoral praxis.

McCord Adams' Stage I:

Unity is discovered within a fragmented attention. Division thus accompanies incarnation. God's divine concentration fills divergence. Concentration presupposes trust, at least for the moment. Trust stands for retract in full connection. A pre-lingual level of consciousness interacts in invisible threads with speech. Transformation, adaptation on the road to expression within time has been fulfilled. Similarly, untouchable threads between suffering people and God's absence connect what appears to diverge. Invisible unity rarely manifests itself. Its shallow traces signify freedom. The power of personal statements is effective in political speech. In religion, a combination of words and acts is necessary for divine effectiveness. Hence, these words are vulnerable declarations.

Vulnerability requires justice. Oneness presupposes order in diversion. Though, in digression, disorder may appear. Trust in Oneness makes vulnerable to scepticism. Pragmatism is more profitable. Nevertheless, it is in this niche of helpless *demasqué* that the symbol of the cross demonstrates its power as a *skandalon*. It may transform dullness to an 'intimate, personal, and overall beatific relationship with God'. In many aspects, the cross of the Christians became an intense cross. It puzzles me since years if and how invisible threads of organic unity are to be traced. How difficult is it to be patient, and to see what happens. Fundamentalism opts for quick exclusiveness. The cross of diversity accordingly is a curse. McCord's invitation to welcome a vision on healing still sounds firm and remote from 'disabled voluntarism'. It reminds me again of Augustine's inclusion of powerful vulnerability within a kenotic perspective. Yet, without social Trinity.

3.4 Did Augustine's Word incarnate speak its unity within two minds?

Somehow and somewhere, *Logos-Sarx* Christology became a hallmark for orthodox Christianity. Though, in the previous sections it was noticed that kenotic perspectives had a strong influence on theology, particularly in dialogue with liberation movements and ecological theology, the metaphor of a self-emptying God is still moving the hearts of many socially engaged Christian projects. In Augustine, both perspectives merged into a theology of wisdom. In Christ, Wisdom incarnated a divine method. Fusion of both perspectives in Christ qualified Augustine to make horrors of human existence participate in a vision of hope and perfection.

In recent decades, many authors in philosophical theology have taken Chalcedonian Christology as their point of reference, for better or for worse. John Hick criticized Chalcedonian Christology because of its universalistic claims. Herman Philipse and Daniel Dennett both blamed Christian doctrine for incoherency. In reaction, urged by debate in philosophy of religion, other authors aimed for a position to investigate whether and how essential elements of doctrine (Trinity!) can be understood in coherence with Scripture as well as with sound logic. For most of them, analytical philosophical methods were regular instruments in their philosophical toolboxes. The so-called *logical desiderata* for major concepts of deity, incarnation, atonement, Trinity, omnipotence, omniscience and goodness have been set up. In subsequent debates, these were reviewed critically.

The doctrine on a divine-human Jesus Christ touches both anthropology and the doctrine of the Trinity. Hence, a vivid debate on Christology emerged in 1988. It was published in the book *Encountering Jesus. A Debate on Christology,* edited by Stephen T. Davis. This book was modelled after Rabbinic Talmud debate. Thus, a variety of theologians reacted to contemporary Christology. Contributions that have inspired me for the purpose of this book were particularly those from John Hick (pluralism), John Cobb (process theology), Stephen Davis (evangelical orthodoxy, Chalcedonian Christology), Rebecca Pentz (feminism) and Michael Wyschogorod (Jewish). In a broader sense, not only Alvin Plantinga but also Thomas Morris have contributed intensively to this debate. All these authors share their intention to convey an account of essential Christian doctrine which can be defended as coherent, or at least not incoherent. Yet, they differ in their respective approaches and methods pertaining to the concept of unity.

This said, it is time to return to Augustine's seventh book of *Confessions:* his rejection of Platonic pride. Rowan Williams' analysis of this passage will be immensely helpful to assess Augustine's text in the background of a contrasting view of Thomas Morris on Christ and Trinity. Firstly, I draw attention to Thomas Morris' defeat of the standard kenotic model of Christology. Later in this section, I refer to his thesis of a two-mind perspective on the person of Christ and I will return to Augustine's merged perspective of divine unity. Thus, the lead of Morris' argument for a refined model of social Trinity offers an incentive to re-read Augustine's discussion on Platonic pride in *Confessions.*

In his book, *The Logic of the God incarnate*, Thomas Morris reacted to a debate on incarnation. Its motivation was a response to Nicolas Lash's wake-up call for 'a fresh look at the logical problems to which classical formulations in Christology give rise' (Lash, 1979, 42). After its publication, the book was reviewed. The conclusion was that 'all the hard-logical work yet remains to be done' (Keith Ward, reviewing Lash in *Theology*, 1979). Even though highly demanding for his readers, Morris' publication was of great service. He made hotspots from the subsequent debates in philosophical theology accessible for a broader theological audience in *The Logic of the God incarnate*. He focussed on four major problems: firstly, the charge on Christian doctrine of incoherence in Christological concepts. This complaint took the claim of numerical identity of the historical Jesus with the Son in Trinity into account. A second problem was a charge of incoherence between modern cosmology and incarnation. Universalism in salvation for cosmic forms of life and process theology were leading topics in this debate. A third problem was related to religious epistemology. How do we know whether incarnation happened? Morris preferred kenotic models in his analysis of process theology. He thus claimed to be able to liberate process theology from the *indictum* not to respect God's freedom in creation. A closing chapter on Trinitarian theology tailors the arguments of his book into a defence of Chalcedonian's definition in Christology.

Back to Augustine: his assertion that nothing but Christ's humility can heal pride, in *Confessions* VII.9.13-14, is more than a simplistic correction for the omission of Christ's name. Rowan Williams' article 'Augustine's Christology: Its Spirituality and Rhetoric' (Williams 2008) proposed a multi-layered analysis of this fragment. From the outset, Rowan Williams recognized how Augustine's explanation for the omission of Christ's name was significantly explained with the help of Paul's hymn on Christ: Phil. 2.7-11. Augustine criticized them (the Platonists) for focussing excessively on divine aspects of the Christ. 'Although they knew God, yet they glorify Him not as God, nor are thankful, but wax vain in their thoughts; and their foolish heart is darkened; professing that they were wise, they became fools' (*Conf.* VII.9.14).

In Chapter 2, I have mentioned Augustine's merge of Johannine divine presence and kenotic Pauline reflection: a safe route to integrate imperfection in universal salvation. Wisdom had corroborated his position in the text on the *libri platonicorum* from *Confessions*. It was preceded by a passage pointing out how a kenotic perspective supports the prospect of Christ as *sapientia* (Williams 2008, 177).

Rowan Williams' conclusion is that unity in speech and act in life constitute Jesus' *simplum* which integrated *duplum* of division. Its unity transformed Jesus' person. Hence, effects of the self-emptying act of humility can be detected all over the process of incarnation. Williams observed a shift in Augustine's understanding of *sapientia* around AD 390. Increasingly profound reflection on the Bible made Augustine's pattern of Christ as 'Reason' more open for what appeared as unreasonable from Scripture. 'Humble acceptance of God's accommodation to our condition correlates with the understanding of divine humility as the unifying foundation for all God's revealing work' (Williams 2008, 186–7). Humility thus labelled Augustine's stance towards the domain of senses, and consequential division. It was precisely this type of humility that Augustine missed in Platonist books. Accordingly, Augustine identified humility with a self-emptying God.

Before we proceed to Thomas Morris' kenotic Christology, for the sake of memory, I return to the first part of the fragment from *Conf.* VII.9.13:

And Thou, willing first to show me how Thou resistest the proud, but givest grace unto the humble, and by how great an act of Thy mercy Thou hadst traced out to men the way of humility, in that Thy Word was made flesh, and dwelt among men: Thou procuredst for me, by means of one puffed up with most unnatural pride, certain books of the Platonists, translated from Greek into Latin. And therein I read, not indeed in the very words, but to the very same purpose, enforced by many and divers reasons, that In the beginning was the Word, and the Word was with God, and the Word was God: the Same was in the beginning with God: all things were made by Him, and without Him was nothing made: that which was made by Him is life, and the life was the light of men, and the light shineth in the darkness, and the darkness comprehended it not. And that the soul of man, though it bears witness to the light, yet itself is not that light; but the Word of God, being God, is that true light that lighteth every man that cometh into the world. And that He was in the world, and the world was made by Him, and the world knew Him not. But, that He came unto His own, and His own received Him not; but as many as received Him, to them gave He power to become the sons of God, as many as believed in His name; this I read not there. (*Conf* VII.9.13, transl. Pusey)

Three points came to the fore from the reading of this text in Chapter 2. Firstly, it was observed that Augustine's theology on Christ as the divine Word was balanced in Paul's kenotic hymn in Phil. 2.6-7. From the follow-up of this fragment in Chapter 2, it was demonstrated that Augustine deliberately added words to the scriptural text that refer to Nicene theology of unity. Secondly, I have commented on Augustine's deliberations about the omission of the glorified Word in the Platonic books. Thirdly, attention was drawn on Augustine's discussion of the virtue of humility in contrast with pride.

This said, it is time to return to Thomas Morris. Apparently, Augustine's preference for the antithesis humility–pride shows parallels with Morris' inclination towards kenotic Christology. Yet, Thomas Morris epitomized Augustine's attitude, dominated by unity. Augustine was mentioned in Morris' book a few times, in the context of process theology. Hence, Morris' criticism: it 'tends to see the threeness of the Trinity as merely three modes of the existence of one individual being' (Morris 1986, repr. 2001, 212). In Morris' view, a (patristic) social view on Trinity is a sound context for process philosophy, liberating from accusations of unorthodoxy. Though, criticism was raised that process theology was not able to respect adequately God's freedom in the act of creation. Thus, matter and time are contingent (Morris 1986, repr. 2001, 210–18).

In a first response to Morris' account on Augustine's position, the latter's orientation of Platonic pride in *Confessions* VII directs the attention to reasons for the use of Nicene Trinitarian terminology on unity of substance. Still, it was elucidated that Augustine believed the person of Christ was a merge of divine and human, without mingling. A kenotic approach helped him to balance between divine presence and participation. On the other hand, Nicene concepts made him avoid disunity.

Morris' characterization of Augustine as a theologian who represented a theory which 'tends to see the threeness of Trinity as merely three modes of existence of one individual being' makes the impression of one-sidedness. While Morris was correct in his observations of Augustine's preference for unity, he neglected Augustine's frequent exegesis of kenotic scriptural narrative. Moreover, Morris' description of a contrast between Augustine's theology of unity and social Trinitarianism voiced by Cappadocian fathers overlooked Augustine's complex intellectual history. Unfortunately, it happened more than once that Augustine's reception pinpointed him with predicates which did not cover the complexity of his theology.

More convincing is Morris' dissatisfaction with examples of extreme kenotic Christology he had found in nineteenth-century theology. Radical views found their incentive in a claim that Jesus divested himself from distinctive metaphysical attributes while becoming human. All the same, Jesus remained in the possession of moral qualities from divine origen. Divine attributes, such as omnipotence, omniscience and necessity, pertain to ontological qualities. Moral qualities referred to Jesus' holiness. Thomas Morris argued that this specific type of kenotic Christology requires social Trinitarianism in some form. The latter allows to conceive 'the Trinity as consisting in three metaphysically distinct individuals severally exemplifying the attributes of deity [...] a society of divine persons' (Morris 1986, repr. 2001, 92). Nevertheless, Jesus' ability, while being human to continue divine activity in connection with creation, was an interesting test case for Morris to avoid polytheism.

The concept of simultaneous creation over time and his theology of the *totus Christus* helped Augustine to solve this Christological conundrum. Augustine did not merely defend the Word created 'in the beginning'. Moreover, he explained its activity sustained over time and in life-giving force. Thus, creation was sustained in its continuity while Jesus existed as a human person. The *totus Christus* figure expressed unity vigorously. It was stabilized in kenotic exegesis and closely related to humility. All the same, Augustine's humility was not synonymous with powerlessness. Pride rules out seeing the truth. Ever since Platonism was exclusive because of its intellectual nature, humble acceptance of the name of Christ is a remedy, accessible to all who search for it.

Thomas Morris constructed a two-mind theory as a better alternative to radical kenotic Christology. He distinguished two levels of consciousness within the person of Christ. The most abstract level is 'the eternal mind of God the Son with its distinctively divine consciousness' (Morris 1986, repr. 2001, 103). On the other side, there is 'a distinctly earthly consciousness that came into existence and grew and developed as the boy Jesus grew and developed' (Morris 1986, repr. 2001, 103). These two levels were in 'an asymmetrical accessing relationship'. Thus, Morris avoided conflicts with the scriptural account of the youth of Jesus. Along these lines, Morris escaped docetic, Apollinarian and Nestorian errors. Analogies from psychology (subconscious, conscious) and research data from hemisphere commissurotomy patients corroborated Morris' model. These patients gave testimonials that indicate synergy of different types of consciousness within the same person (Morris 1986, repr. 2001, 105). In his sermons, Augustine revealed a remarkable interest in medicine and medical metaphors. However, no references to brain-surgery were made. Though, distinctions between conscious and a form of subconscious activity were mentioned in Augustine's reflections on dreams, and on sense perception. Additionally, he studied the effects of misleading optical images in contrast with the vision of God in interiority. An asymmetrical relationship between divine and human levels of consciousness thus became distinctive for Morris' Christology.

Hence, Morris discussed divine presence within Jesus in the context of incarnation. Yet, in this setting, many objections have been raised inspired by the Anselmian thesis of God's necessary goodness. On the proposition that God omnipotent necessary must be free and able to do evil, Morris replied that 'Traditional theists who hold this belief intuitively, or infer it from more general beliefs or principles they hold intuitively, can be justified in taking such intuitions to be reliable and in maintaining there exist no defeaters of those intuitions' (Morris 1986, repr. 2001, 135–6). Hence, for Morris, justification of belief is a posteriori activity. Creation testifies in signs and miracles. It parallels the Nicodemian *modus tollens*: 'Rabbi, we know that you are a teacher come from God; for no man can do these signs that you do unless God is with him' (Jn 3.1-2). Morris thus concluded: 'there seems to be no obstacle in principle to the acceptability of the widespread Christian assumption that it is possible that it is rational to believe that Jesus to be God incarnate' (Morris 1986, repr. 2001, 204).

How does this rationale link up with Augustine's plea for humility? Certainly, both Augustine and Thomas Morris repeatedly employed kenotic theology. Most likely, Morris' concern for coherence in theology of creation and incarnation would have invoked Augustine's positive consideration. Though, the social models of Trinity that were corroborated by Morris probably may have made him hesitate, or even rejective. In Augustine's theology of Trinity, it is the metaphor of *imago Dei* that accomplished the task of mediation between divine and human in creation. Pride and original sin accordingly have wounded human moral capabilities. The Son's action of self-humiliation rescued humankind. Morris agreed that salvation demands universality. Though, for Augustine, universal salvation was affirmed in human anthropology: 'And that the soul of man, though it bears witness to the light, yet itself is not that light; but the Word of God, being God' (*Conf* VII.9.3). In the follow-up of his argument, the upshot was that intellectual pride blocked Platonists from intellectual vision. Humble revelation thus cures pride and can make fools wise. Still, Augustine knew there was *massa damnata*.

The efforts of Morris' intellectual tour de force may well match up with Augustine's own inclination to validate human intellect positively. While wounded and weakened, the limits of intellect had been tested in Augustine's own efforts to understand Scripture and theological concepts coherently. Nonetheless, *On Trinity* and other treatises regularly ended up in apophatic exclamations.

In sum, Morris distanced himself from unitarian theories of Trinity and from the Christology he had identified with Augustine. Nevertheless, he shared more with the bishop of Hippo than appeared at first glance. Thus, Augustine's account of the divine presence of the Word in the human Jesus finds a counterpart in Morris' concern for contingency of creation. God is free; God is almighty; God has become incarnate.

Personal reflection

Morris' two-mind theory on Jesus appeals to the common sense of Bible readers. The narratives of the Gospels invite us to identify with Jesus. Whether he was curing the sick, or unified with his Father in heaven, readers often sympathize with Christ. Once the perspective of the One has been adopted, it becomes effective throughout all reading. Depraved senses are healed; absence creates meaning. Morris' message is clear. However, his argumentations require skilled readers. Not all Bible readers are skilled readers. Particularly not in analytic philosophy and formal reasoning. Our fragmented age asks for non-esoteric solutions.

Marilyn McCord Adams' horror defeating, stage II:

I see many people planning seriously to engage in the narrative of meaning. Though, engagement requires attention. Patristic texts reflect the multiplicity of engagements in early Christian theology. Yet, it is an urgent task for patristic scholars to bring the terms of engagement for the fore. In no way, unity excuses to refrain from action in situations of injustice. On the contrary, insight on organic unity includes justice for the benefit of all: the race for the vaccine and access to it. Thus, healed from short-sightedness and quick 'solutions', justice corresponds to order. Though, order requires unity, rather than two minds.

3.5 Does Augustine's resurrected body meet humanity's expectations?

The perspective of life surviving bodily death triggers many people. Though, at a growing rate, citizens confess themselves as agnostic on this topic. However, medical sciences have extended the focus of research beyond the preservation of life and health. They have included physiology of dying in recent investigations. Yet, propositions on the possibility of continuing life after bodily disintegration do not have a place in accepted medical research. Still, for many people, survival of the person over decreasing physiological functions of the body continued to attract attention. Identity and individuality have been key concepts in the discussion on possible conditions for life surviving bodily death. In philosophical reflection on *desiderata* of life that survives death, it is crucial that personal identity remains the same after death, as before death.

Augustine's thoughts on the topic of eternal life generally developed in the context of the resurrection of Christ. Not only his Eastern sermons but also contemplations over God's sabbatical rest on the seventh day of creation *(Confessions XIII)* shaped Augustine's apprehension of continuity of life over bodily death. In the end, God perfects moral and bodily imperfection. The Gospels' narrative on the resurrection of Christ was a most important model. It helped him to conceive individual existence after death. And yet,

Platonic insights on the soul and its relation to the body facilitated him to articulate ideas on afterlife and resurrection in the context of philosophical anthropology. Accordingly, ambiguity between embodied perfection and angelic existence remained persistent in Augustine's work. In *The City of God,* Augustine quoted biblical testimonials on Jesus' apparitions within the group of disciples. He still wore his wounds (Thomas!). He was able to eat but did not permit people to touch Him (Mary of Magdala). Otherwise, Augustine clarified how the body was renewed, perfected and destined for eternal life in the bliss of the vision of God.

To review this aspect of Augustine's theology more in detail, I return to his findings on resurrection at the end of *The City of God,* XII.14-17. In this fragment, in line with Paul's letter to the Romans, he conveyed that the human body will be perfected in conformity with the image of God. Along these lines, he did not hesitate to summarize some details on bodily resurrection. He included the concept of perfect measure. It envisaged accomplishment as well as ambiguity in his view on resurrection.

Life that survives death has been studied renewed in anthropology and philosophy of religion. Trenton Merricks is known as a physicalist. He published on metaphysics and likewise wrote on the topic of resurrection. He argued for consistency within the doctrine of resurrection. Though, it was his contention that there is only one model: physical resurrection (Trenton Merricks, 'The Resurrection of the Body', Rea and Flint 2009, 476).

Some initial annotations are to be made: Firstly, Augustine's account on the 'age' of the resurrected body in Christological perspective mentions the number of thirty-three. Even children, died at young age, will rise in a resurrected body of a thirty-three-year-old person. Trenton Merricks argued for physical resurrection. In his view it is the only prospect to make sense of incarnation without doctrinal inconsistencies. Augustine's account of the resurrected person mentioned bodily details that bring the risen Jesus present to the mind: wounds, sharing food after resurrection with disciples, visibility in a risen body. Yet, Augustine included signs and language in his perspective on salvation: Scriptural exegesis and restoration of peace within justice.

We are left, therefore, with one conclusion, namely, that each of us will have that size we had in our maturity, even though we die in extreme old age; or we shall have that size we would have had in our maturity, in case we died earlier. Hence, we must interpret St. Paul's words concerning 'the mature measure of the fullness of Christ' as meaning, for example, that the measure of His fullness will be reached when all of His members, the Christian people, will have been added to Christ the Head; or the words may mean, if they have reference to the resurrection, that all will rise with bodies neither less nor larger than the size of their mature age, and so in the age and vigour of thirty years-since that is the age reached by Christ and the age which even secular authorities consider the age of mature manhood and the age beyond which a man declines toward the weakness of old age. That is why St. Paul did not speak of the measure either of the body or of the stature but of 'the measure of the age of the fullness of Christ.' (*CG* XXII.15, transl. Walsh)

Secondly, Augustine's *desideratum* for inclusion and participation of suffering within God's order: words and sacraments. In modelling the process of human liberation after the *totus Christus*, Augustine implanted solidarity in suffering. Merricks' assessment of resurrection focussed on logical consistency, rather than on moral or ethical implications. In distinction with Augustine, less attention was paid to communal aspects of resurrection. However, he briefly addressed the community of saints and their intercession of prayer. At the end of his article, he concluded:

So I suspect that, whatever we say about the existence of human beings between death and resurrection, any petitions that reach the saints do so by 'going through God' in some way or other. But once we concede this, I see nothing objectionable about the mechanism I have suggested. And that mechanism is consistent with each saint – like each of us – jumping ahead in time from his or her death to the Day of Resurrection. (Merricks 2009), in Rea and Flint 2009, 486)

In Augustine's account at the end of *The City of God*, book XXII, the community of saints is the foundation of celestial Jerusalem. For the bishop of Hippo, the existence of this heavenly community warranted a successful horror-defeating process in completion of sufferings and wounds of the saints (see the previous section: McCord Adams).

Thirdly, Augustine's outline of resurrected life has been described as 'angelic' (Andrea Nightingale: *Once out of Nature: Augustine on Time and the Body*). In eschatological situation, metaphysical orientation is directed towards bliss and vision: a dissolution of marriage. Genital organs function corresponding to will. Thus, an ascetic delineation of resurrection was drawn in Augustine's *The City of God*. A stark contrast with Trenton Merricks' physicalist picture of resurrected life emerges. Still, in Augustine's *The City of God*, risen people have abilities to eat, to speak and to walk in resurrected bodies of perfect age and measure. Embodiment thus indicates metaphysical goodness of created matter in contrast with Manichean dualism. Yet, 'the mature measure of the fullness of Christ' represented bodily as well as spiritual salvation in its completion. Augustine:

> The text of St. Paul which speaks of the saints predestined to become conformed to the image of his Son is susceptible of two interpretations. It may refer to the purely interior man [. . .] A second interpretation is that we are to be 'conformed' to Him in immortality, as He was conformed to us in our mortality. And, in this sense, the test refers to the resurrection of our bodies. However, we must remember that, even in this interpretation, the 'conformity' is no more a matter of the size of our bodies in the resurrection than the 'measure' in the other text refers to size. It is a matter of maturity. All are to have, in the resurrection, the mature bodies they had, or would have had, in the maturity of their manhood. However, it would really make no difference to have, in form, a child's or an old man's body, since there is to be no weakness of soul nor even any infirmity in body. And so, if anyone cares to defend the position that we are to rise with the same shaped body we had at death, there is nothing to be gained by pursuing the debate. (*CG* XXII.16)

Andrea Nightingale's conclusion that Augustine's picture of human was angelic and 'out of nature' is confusing. Even in the early stages of his career, Augustine's preference to stage the setting of his pedagogy with examples from material reality became apparent in

On the Happy Life. Although, a leading assertion in *On the Happy Life* was denial of full happiness within time and matter. Yet, daily exercises in virtuous life can make a person receptive for measure and order. Thus, happiness in its incomplete form provides the path towards bliss and vision.

Yet, at this instant there remains more to discuss on Trenton Merricks. His first major book was *Objects and Persons* in 2001. In this publication, he discussed metaphysics of entities in categories of simples. These simples have been arranged as objects. Merricks by and large adheres to a refined nihilist view. He asserted that only material simples exist. However, together with Peter van Inwagen, he made an exception for the category of life. This takes especially the human person into account, as she is capable to exercise free will. Consciousness is an intrinsic phenomenon. It does not exclusively supervene on micro-biological activities and is not relational (Merricks 2001, 103). Specifically, in his defence of free will and in his minimalistic theory of relations between parts and wholes (mereology), fascinating aspects of the resurrection came to the fore.

In his contribution to the *Oxford Handbook of Philosophical Theology*, Trenton Merricks paid ample attention to the 'how' and the 'why' of resurrection (Merricks 2009 in Rea and Flint 2009, 476–90). Expounding on 'why-questions' in the section on Body and Person, Merricks discussed the Apostles Creed: '[I believe in] the resurrection of the body, and the life everlasting. It was his contention to demonstrate in a three-staged argument that we are identical with our bodies' (Ibid. 483–4). Step 1: Each of us has physical properties. Step 2: Each of us is located where our body is located. Step 3: There is one object exactly and entirely located and one object with all of the physical properties had by a person and her body. Therefore, we are identical with our bodies.

Merricks ironically reasoned that, since dead bodies cease to exist, people who confess the Apostles Creed have a difficult task to explain the transition to bodily resurrection after death (Ibid. 484–5). Still, Merricks argued 'that we are identical with our bodies because this identity makes the best sense of a specifically Christian claim surrounding life after death, even life after the destruction of one's body' (Ibid. 484–5). On subject matter of the 'how' question on resurrection of the body, Merricks referred to change and temporal gaps. Change, because every human body grows, and shifts in shape and size since childhood. Identity remains one and the same throughout the process of growth.

The doctrine of resurrection implies that a body shall rise and exist again. Thus, a temporal gap between a body that has deceased and the risen body ask for explanation. Within this temporal gap, an account of identity of the deceased-and-risen person is necessary. Merrick mentioned two explanations: a general reassembly account and an early rabbinic account. In the assembly model, Merricks argued for a universal reconstruction of extinct bodies. The rabbinic theory suggests that the body will be reconstructed around a bone that is indestructible. Since no indestructible bones remain after cremation, Merricks concluded that the soul will not be able to warrant identity over death. 'Some might suggest that my current body will be identical with whatever resurrection body has the same (*substantial*) soul as is had by my current body. But a soul is not part of a body' (Ibid. 479).

This is a fascinating account on resurrection, which represents a contrasting view on Augustine's exposé on nature and essence of the human soul. In the second chapter, Augustine's evaluation of Paul's theology of resurrection was discussed: that (saintly) humans will be 'conformed to the image of the Son'. Hence, a risen body will be perfected. It can expect liberation from illnesses and defects. It will be perfected in conformity to 'the mature measure of the fullness of Christ'. Then again, how bodily is this perfected body? Augustine contended that 'the measure of His fullness will be reached when all of His members, the Christian people, will have been added to Christ the Head' (*CG* XXII.15). In Augustine's view, perfection will be accomplished only in the end. All members of the *totus Christus* will have experienced recollection within eschaton: *apokatastasis*. Completion thus is not yet finished at the moment a body dies and is going to disintegrate. In Augustine, as well as in Merricks' theory, identity of a person survives until the moment of final accomplishment. Augustine argued that the risen body will acquire a perfect measure of a 33-year-aged body. Consequently, the risen body is perfect in measure. Hence, simultaneously it is a glorified body.

Augustine's heavenly body lingers in ambivalence: risen and embodied. Merricks' resurrected body is purely bodily in its constitution: no ambiguity. Accordingly, Trenton Merricks' theory on Trinity and the relationship between humans and God focussed on the concept of person in his article 'Split Brains and the Godhead'

(Merricks 2006). In this contribution, Merricks argued against merely social concepts of Trinity (Ibid. 305–8). He conceded that 'Social trinitarianism is the view that it is important, for theological and pastoral purposes, to articulate and emphasize the love and other social relationships among the persons of the Trinity' (Ibid. 2006, 308). But 'Social trinitarians need not – must not – defend the pure theory. So, they must allow that more than love unites the divine persons. But social trinitarianism as such does not say what this more is'. Hence, Merricks cannot be coined as a kenotic theologian.

> He continued: the social Trinitarian cannot accuse us of modalism if we defend the claim that there are three divine persons in what she takes to be the relevant sense of 'person' (Ibid. 318). Hence, Trenton Merricks persisted the sceptical side of argument. He concluded that he failed to have 'proven that the Doctrine, rightly interpreted, is not contradictory. But such a proof is not the only way to defend the Doctrine from the charge of contradiction. One could, instead, argue that there is no compelling reason to believe the Doctrine is contradictory. It is this sort of defense I have presented.' (Ibid. 324)

Personal reflection

Merricks' line of reasoning on resurrection is maximally physicalist as well as minimally metaphysical. It is minimal, even though vigorous reason provides a foundation for knowledge of the most unknown: the nature of the human self. Augustine went on a different track. He framed his knowledge in old words: a provocative narrative. On the pulpit, he uttered old words. Though, he trusted God's speech in time. He trusted hermeneutical complexity to a maximum. In contrast, Merricks' account on resurrection relied on 'what minimally can contended' without being in contradiction.

Scepticism leads to minimalism. Within the minim of metaphysics that is required to secure that we are 'no longer vulnerable to horrors', ideals may become detached from daily life. They are closed for the have-nots. Yet, consistency appeals to a select group of highly motivated searchers. Augustine's theory is embodied and intentionally accessible, even in deliberations on the risen body.

Thus, I see that scriptural texts have difficulty in attracting persistent attention of contemporary readers. Neither is their authority self-evident.

McCord Adams, Stage III:

In recreating relationship with material world, the basis of minimalist and sound reason may convince a small group of professionals. Though, it is mostly the class of maximalist narratives that provides consolation and healing to the many. Along these lines, I see it as providential that minimalist people explain what may be certain in moments of doubt and exhaustion. It is also providence that storytellers such as Augustine once crossed my path. As a student, I was caught in the loops of his sentences. Still, I seek for the person and the intentions of Augustine's biblical reasoning.

3.6 Conclusion

Three divergent readings from Augustine and contemporary theologians pondered on Jesus from three different perspectives. They have demonstrated that, despite contrasts and mutual criticisms, there is common ground. In the first section on kenosis, Marilyn McCord Adams' criticism of Augustine's 'disabled voluntarism' sounds pertinent. And yet, in the first section of this chapter I argued that Augustine's kenotic exegesis of the book of Genesis probably matches requirements for McCord Adams' three-stage horror-defeat model. Her wish to participate in restoration of meaning-creating capacities was basically fulfilled with Augustine's integration of suffering within the self-emptying incarnation, adapted to the weaknesses of humanity: *congruentia*.

A second section on *Logos-Sarx* Christology in Augustine's *Confessions VII* focussed on humility and pride. It contrasted with the work of Thomas Morris on social Trinity and kenosis. Rowan Williams' analysis of Augustine's *Confessions* and second book of *On Trinity* directed the reading to the concept of humility. Morris' two-mind theory appeals to modern readers. So does his analysis of research on lobotomy patients. Though, this approach is in disparity with Augustine's apophatic stance in the closing book of *On Trinity*. Augustine's high appraisal of non-esoterism and humility does not easily match with specialist knowledge from neurology.

The third section of this chapter was engaged with the risen human person as described in Augustine's *The City of God* and in Trenton Merricks' physicalist perspective. While minimalistic in its sceptical stance, Merricks argued for a theory on Trinity that aimed on what *is* more than relationship. Even though Trenton Merricks' theory pointed towards a minimum of maximally trustworthy knowledge, he also claimed a high Christology in agreement with Chalcedon. Augustine's view on the resurrected person was embodied. Though, it retained some ambiguity. Thus, in the closing book of *The City of God*, the resurrected human rises within a measure of perfection. Yet, Trenton Merricks' account on resurrection remained purely embodied.

Presently, physicalism is mainstream in sciences and major areas of philosophical anthropology. Though, theological doctrine regained attention from philosophical theology. Despite a host of differences, some of them support in some form that a defence of Chalcedonian Christology is possible without logical incoherence.

Augustine's picture of Christ advertises piety in coherence. Though, his opinions were underpinned by scriptural reasoning. Authority speaks, but reason makes distinctions. Its conjectures regard the self and God. Despite the many differences and even incoherencies between Augustine's associative style of reasoning, and the *desiderata* from contemporary philosophical discourse, it must be noticed that on many sides common ground exists between the authors we have discussed in this chapter: a preference for kenotic narrative. They appeal to the contemporary search for recognizable and rhetorically effective expressions of religious life. Our digital age wrestles with complex relationships between virtual reality and corporeal presence in time and matter. Augustine's picture of resurrection is obviously embodied. Yet, for contemporary naturalists, the Augustinian picture of the risen body sketches an ascetic perspective that does not meet all standards. Hence, there are topics for a dialogue in the next chapter on embodied CSR and Augustine's theology of healing in perfection.

4

Christology in dialogue

Augustine and philosophical theology on the human body

4.1 Religion and science: Patristics in dialogue with brain science?

Religion and science have maintained an intense, but steady relationship. Religious leaders can't keep away from dialogue without losing stature. Yet, many of them invite exchange of ideas. Some of them confuse it with monologue. In science, it is common practice that religion and personal conviction are strictly separated from arguments. Names from history recall a tensed liaison between science and religion: Nicolaus Copernicus, Isaac Newton, David Hume's *Natural History of Religion* (1757) and his *Dialogues Concerning Natural Religion* (1779; published posthumously).

Still, in the last three decades, interdisciplinary research in cognitive science of religion has made germane contributions to a renewed understanding of religion. Input from cognitive psychology, cognitive neuroscience, computer science, linguistics, anthropology and philosophy induced a multifaceted revival in the study of religion. Mostly, these scholars refer to religion as a natural phenomenon. It emerged in evolution. Though, functional analysis of religion incited the theory that religion developed to cope with cooperative and social tasks in evolution. Thus, religions as overarching systems were linked to evolutionary stages of human development, especially when the groups where human beings worked and lived in, enlarged.

An additional branch of CSR has made major progress as a result of insights from neurology. These discernments were shared among interdisciplinary research groups founded in the last decade before the second millennium. Armin Geertz was an outstanding pioneer. Topics such as prehistory of the mind, functions of counter-intuitive agencies in religious practice and rituals were prominent in the debates of the new discipline.

A variety of theories and models emerged. In critical realism, J. Wentzel van Huyssteen aimed for a moderate form of dialogue between biology and theology. Since this perspective goes well along with kenotic theology, it has received much attention. Though, criticism considered van Huyssteen's theory incompatible with Chalcedonian Christianity. Others, such as Alvin Plantinga, contended that major controversies were not between religion and science. Instead, he mentioned the antithesis between naturalism and theology. As a result, scholars from philosophy of religion and philosophical theology studied renewed anthropological concepts. However, methodological disparities between philosophical theology (analytic) and CSR (inductive) made this type of interdisciplinary research not self-evident. Though, I will argue in this chapter for the inclusion of dialogue within philosophical theology. I see this chapter as an experiment in this type of dialogue. Recent debate encompassed topics such as *imago Dei* (e.g. Structural Image of God) and the hypothesis of a *sensus divinitatis* (Hyper Active Agency Detection Device).

Since the seventeenth century, church leaders' response to questions on religion and science frequently was quiet or reacted against modernism. Though, since the twentieth century, major efforts were made invigorating dialogue between science and religions. In Roman Catholic circles, religious orders such as Jesuits, Dominicans and Augustinians have been active in the arenas of scholarship and education. In Islamic theology, the history of dialogue on faith and reason goes back to Maimonides' *Guide of the Perplexed*. In Buddhistic theology, separation between philosophy and religion never was observed in detail. Though, in our days, it must be noticed that responses from theology on CSR have been meagre until yet. Methodological matters prematurely have been set aside in separatist perspectives on theology and science. Since dialogue as a practice in doing philosophy has firm roots in history, it is my aim to try out how dialogue between Augustine and CSR may add to philosophical theology. Yet, in the recent past, major contributions have been made: the concept of nature, perceived as a book of God. Along these lines, science functions as an empirical method for enquiry, while theology offers a signifying framework. A supplementary point of view was stipulated by natural theology. In this discipline, cosmological arguments and *a priori* arguments with an intention to prove God's existence paved the way for a discussion on philosophical presuppositions for a Structural Image of God (Aku Visala – Helen De Cruz). Traditional *imago Dei*-theology was criticized for its tendency to give priority to intellectual capacities over bodily aspects. Thus, in his article 'Imago Dei, Dualism, and Evolution: A Philosophical Defense of the Structural Image of God', Aku Visala questioned criticism on *imago Dei*-theology. He proposed a refined version of a Structural Image of God-model. This model defined the body as that which makes the human person completely humanly. Visala thus deflated critical assessments of *imago Dei*-theories from natural theology (De Smedt and de Cruz 2014; Olli-Pekka Vainio 2014). Aku Visala argued that 'the image of God is as much about being as it is about becoming' (Visala 2014a, 118). Hence, he endorsed renewed attention for refined *imago Dei*-theories. These theories 'can identify the *imago Dei* with the developing of certain dispositions and capacities when the organisms in question are properly functioning'.

A different but productive perspective on religion emerged from interdisciplinary research on brain processes and religious experience. Ilkka Pyysiäinen and Armin Geertz harvested the fruits of fundamental work from neurologist Antonio Damasio. Impressively, Pyysiäinen in *How Religion Works* (2003) aimed for a comprehensive theory of religion. Armin Geertz determined himself to study religion with special attention for embodied contexts of religious practices. Thus, he argued that methods of redundant rituals in sacred spaces that invoke emotional states and memories of them deserve to be studied with more attention in theological debate.

CSR scholars' judgements on religion separate into two strands. An influential fraction sympathizes with the thesis that religion emerged during evolutionary selection and therefore was functional. Others see religion as a by-product of natural cognitive capacities. Religion thus eventually came to the light from neurological brain routes that have shaped religious practice. Accordingly, in their view, religious behaviour reflects functional properties of neurological structures.

Functional analysis of religion has strong roots in nineteenth-century sociology. Émile Durkheim assessed religion first and foremost according to its institutional function. Social coherence and ethical motivation were mentioned as distinguishing functions of religious institutions. Since psychology's behaviouristic turn, religion was studied as a phenomenon that motivates human behaviour. Though, investigations that focussed on religions as systems that organize cognition had to wait until Armin Geertz incited renewed attention for (brain) embodied context of religion.

In methodology, CSR scholars share an evidence-based inductive attitude. On the whole, this aspect of research matches not evidently with common hermeneutical methods in theological investigation. Hence, many theologians have decided to leave insights from CSR aside. Vice versa, many CSR scholars dismissed systematic theology as speculative and void. I agree with Geertz that theology has left too many materials unattended. On the other hand, I see that there might be a strong wish to give continuation to attempts from within the discipline of CSR to overcome naturalistic tendencies. Hermeneutical and historical approaches that flourish in patristics are promising partners in dialogue. In Chapter 3, philosophical theology was partner in dialogue. In this chapter, it is my aim to return to Augustine's texts on Christology in the context of issues raised in CSR as an experiment in dialogue within philosophical theology. The familiar threefold perspective of kenosis, *Logos-Sarx* Christology and resurrection will direct the focus of the readings. As in the previous chapters, the issues I have selected for discussion were not representing scholarly urgency. They reflect a personal wish for dialogue in reading Augustine.

In the context of evolutionary biology, the claim has been made that religion should distance itself from the perspective that puts *Homo sapiens* species on top in cosmos. Criticists in this manner opposed to essence-centred models in anthropology. In their view, *Homo sapiens* has evolved over a process of gradual selection. Hence, emergence of *Homo sapiens* species' essence cannot be pinpointed at a distinct moment in time. Accordingly, process theology and doctrinal models that support dynamic cosmology have evolved.

As mentioned before, these theories frequently involved social Trinitarian models. Aspects of relationship consequently delineate interaction between the three divine Persons. Though, orthodox *desiderata* on God's free choice in creation more than once showed themselves incompatible with models of process theology.

4.2 Armin Geertz, Ilkka Pyysiäinen: CSR embodied?

Cultural studies, carried out by anthropologists such as Clifford Geertz, assessed religion in its capacity for cultural transmission and development. Accordingly, many insights on the phenomenology of religion have been won. From 1990 on, comments have been made on reductionist trends in this niche of cultural-anthropological research. As a reaction, CSR scholars reviewed the phenomenon of religion, and aimed to describe specific attributes of religion as a system. Attribution of counter-intuitive properties to objects, agency detection and religions' impressive capacities for transmission of unique knowledge, have since then been resulted in a wealth of publications. For this chapter, I have selected two CSR scholars: Armin Geertz and Ilkka Pyysiäinen. Both the scholars have expressed a keen interest in embodied religion. However, they differ in their respective positions within development of CSR as a discipline.

Armin Geertz spends most of his academic career at Aarhus University. Born in the United States, he moved to Denmark. He dedicated his doctorate research (1992) to Hopi religion: *The Invention of Prophecy: Continuity and Meaning in Hopi Religion.* Though, under influence of increasingly diminishing opportunities to perform field work with the Hopis, he changed focus towards cognition and culture. Thus, propagating an embodied focus on religion, he criticized Clifford Geertz's reductionist evaluation of religion: 'webs of significance'. Foundation of the Toronto journal *Method and Theory in the Study of Religion* (1989) encouraged Armin Geertz to work extensively on method and concepts. Hence, a series of publications reflect his increasingly intensive argument to include relevant disciplines in CSR. Moreover, as a driven CSR prophet, Armin Geertz held many lectures for theologians to explain the relevance of insights that came from CSR for their research. After a period of research on Hopi religion, he became involved in inquiry on New Religious Movements. By and large, Armin Geertz's contention was that religion should be understood as 'a human and cultural product, a kind of overlay in relation to biological, psychological, cultural and social structures and mechanisms' (Geertz 2000, 22). Hence, Geertz aimed to develop an 'anthropological theory, i.e. a theory about the constitution of human beings' (Ibid. 21). He envisaged this type of theory to assess typological schemes that come into view from religious belief. As a track towards explanation of questions raised within research on religion, Armin Geertz drew attention to the relevance of 'secular study of religions by insights achieved in biology, cognitive and cultural psychology, cultural anthropology and sociology' (Ibid. 22).

His advice remained not without consequences. Geertz became personally involved with the *International Association for the Cognitive Science of Religion* (2006). Gradually, the aspect of embodiment became more prominent in Armin Geertz's theory of religion. Particularly the embodied character of cognition – and therefore also of religion – was described as 'anchored in brain and body (embrained and embodied), deeply dependent on culture (enculturated) and extended and distributed beyond the borders of individual brains' (Geertz 2010, 'Brain, Body and Culture: A Biocultural Theory of Religion', 304). Thus, 'religion' should be understood as 'a cultural system and a social institution that governs and promotes ideal interpretations of existence and ideal praxis with reference to postulated transempirical powers or beings' (Geertz 1999, 471). Above all, inclusion of a neurobiological level within the discussion on religion was Geertz's major contribution. The origen of this level was found in expansion of the brain over evolution. Its significance and meaning finds its foundation in neurological somatic schemata that enable to connect mind, brain and body in systematic ways in a broader brain-culture interface. Religion thus formalizes systems of knowledge into schemata. They serve in day-to-day life as meaningful frameworks for action and knowledge. Hence, Armin Geertz's theory on religion goes much beyond Clifford Geertz's webs of significance.

Ilkka Pyysiäinen (Helsinki – Turku) did not limit his research to cognitive aspects of religion. His academic work started with PhD research on mysticism in Indian Buddhism: 'Beyond Language and Reason: Mysticism in Indian Buddhism' (1993). Further in his career, he studied cognition in religion. Particularly, he focussed on the multiform history of the concept 'God' in various religions in recent times and prehistorical past. Hence, in his book *How Religion Works: Towards a New Cognitive Science of Religion* (2003), he combined cognitive research with data from comparative analysis of religions and evolutionary psychology. Along these lines, in his later publication *Supernatural Agents: Why We Believe in Souls, Gods, and Buddhas* (2009), the concept of God represents a class of human thought, rather than a divine, transcendent reality. In this manner, he suggested to reformulate the concept of God. A major point at stake is whether the concept of God is outside all other categories. Or is it a better approach to discuss the concept of God in terms of secular scholarship? Pyysiäinen's response reacted on Durkheim's analysis of religion in terms of social-cultural relationships with other institutions. Pyysiäinen suggested to change track. He propagated to replace symbolic anthropology and structuralism with scholarly study of human cognition and the structures involved. However, in reaction to this approach, criticism aimed on Pyysiäinen's concept of God: it was exclusively related to human cognitive facilities. Without human brain activity, there is no God or social interaction!

Consequently, the phenomenon of religion was studied in its relationship to cross-domain counter-intuitive features. These attributes were ascribed to objects that functioned in religious practices. Within this cross-domain mechanism, neurological domains from several objects and senses are involved. Accordingly, transmission and memorization in religion occurred predominantly with support of counter-intuitive aspects.

Pyysiäinen repeatedly requested attention for the relevance of CSR-based research on behalf of early Christian theology. Hence his 2007 article on resurrection discussed theology's additional relevance ('The Mystery of the Stolen Body: Exploring Christian Origens', Pyysiäinen 2007).

In his assessment of the empty grave in the gospel, Pyysiäinen prepared in analogy with urban legends a mirror narrative. He invented the story of the body of a deceased person in a train. The person was scheduled to be welcomed by a loving family after the journey. When the body unknowingly was removed from the train, the loving family is waiting in vain and searches for the missing body. Along these lines, the start off was made for a story on a missing body. Consequentially, Pyysiäinen discussed a variety of historical explanations for the rise of the story of Jesus' resurrection in early Christianity. Among these, 'it is often claimed that Christianity emerged from the disciples' visions or hallucinations of the risen Christ (Pyysiäinen 2007, 60). On the testimony of Paul, Ilkka Pyysiäinen contended: 'We cannot rule out the possibility that Paul's alleged revelatory experience is only a rhetorical means of legitimating his authority.' Moreover, Ilkka Pyysiäinen argued 'the emergence of Christianity thus cannot be explained without explaining why and how the relevant beliefs were successful in cultural selection; this, in turn, presupposes other arguments in addition to the idea of visions or hallucinations' (Pyysiäinen 2007, 61). In my opinion, this is the perfect moment to bring in theology and its explanation of ideas. Pyysiäinen:

> If the location where Jesus was buried was not known to the disciples, it is quite likely that traditional beliefs about ghosts were activated under proper circumstances (Pyysiäinen 2007, 62) [. . .] Cognitive psychological arguments can help us explain the ways the human mind channels the cultural transmission of religious traditions. Stories of a certain kind become widespread because they have a natural appeal to the human mind. They are attention-grabbing and easy to recall; therefore, they are contagious and get a head start in cultural selection. All kinds of concepts and beliefs compete for our attention; some win and some lose. Those that win are such that somehow 'fit' the human mind, as it were. We cannot help remembering and spreading around the most contagious stories. Cognitive psychology provides tools for finding those features of the mind that channel cultural transmission. (Pyysiäinen 2007, 66)

Accordingly, Pyysiäinen focussed on the mechanisms at work in religion. Instead, inclusion of some exploration on the functions of the theological idea of resurrection in these stories would have offered a valuable contribution to Pyysiäinen's analysis. Thus, in the case of Augustine, the account on Eastern included human suffering within eschatological perspective of healing. The theological idea propounds explanation for religious mechanisms in progress. Leaving this aspect aside leaves an important side of religion unattended. It invites future dialogue!

In anthropology the concept pair emic-etic came to the fore in its analogy to linguistic phonemic and phonetic perspectives. First introduced by Kenneth Pike, *Language in Relation to a Unified Theory of the Structure of Human Behaviour (1954)*, the emic perspective used to investigate human behaviour according to internal indigenous criteria. Hence, an opposing etic perspective affected particularly its capacity to evaluate humanly acting to external criteria. These insights have been productive in the study of cultural materialism, cognitive anthropology and ethnoscience. Despite some refinements that were made on the schemata of emic and etic, a similar division still lingers under postmodernist analysis of culture and religion. And so, the concept pair emic-etic underlined contrasts between regional and global levels of culture and language.

It is tempting to relate these concepts emic-etic to the disciplines of theology and CSR. Yet, in anthropology criticists conveyed that the etic perspective ushered in a connotation of superiority: a scientific stance. In linguistics it became clear that not all of the work that was expected from it was done by the etic perspective. Additionally, it was remarked that culture exists in cultural grammar. 'Rules' thus reign in a community of scholars and cannot warrant for objectively formulated etic perspectives in research. Emic perspectives of anthropological researchers as a group inevitably have left traces in their scholarly products.

Thus, it is manifest that Ilkka Pyysiäinen's approach for investigation of the concept of God (emic) includes unwrapping it from its specific cultural context. What remains is a cross-cultural phenomenon. 'In sum, an etic category of "gods" can only be constructed on the basis of the emic term "god" by dropping the culture-specific contents of "god" and keeping only the cross-cultural core which is formed by the combination of the ideas of agency and counter-intuitiveness' (Pyysiäinen 2003, 21). Accordingly, Pyysiäinen suggested to replace gods with 'counter-intuitive level of reality': 'And, as gods have traditionally been identified as belonging to the transcendent realm, it is now by the same token possible to replace the idea of transcendence, or of the supernatural, by the idea of a counter-intuitive level of reality' (Pyysiäinen 2003, 21–2).

A few remarks on this interesting and provoking thesis are to be made. Firstly, the question is whether and how a concept 'god' that has been dissolved from its culturally specific contents can be conceived or talked over in scholarly debate. Dissolving 'god' from its culturally specific contents doubtless dissolves it from theological contents. All the same, it eventually does associate it with a naturalistic, inductive frame. Further, this purified concept of 'god' leans towards a great common denominator between all emic perspectives (e.g. theology). It voices a higher abstract level of knowledge. What consequences does this bear on our understanding of the concept of 'god'? Shouldn't this concept 'god' not better have pinpointed as 'ᵍᵒᵈ'? It would be tempting to proceed on this track. Along these lines, the concept '···' in infinite 'progressions' leads to unreasonable abstract reflection on religion. If we agree with this, are we able to find relevance in this concept of '···'? Or should we better turn to apophatic mysticism?

Anyway, despite efforts to involve theologians in a dialogue with CSR, it is only a minority within scholarship in early Christianity that has included methods from CSR in their research until yet. The greater part of patristic publications discussed textual interpretations and reflections on doctrinal issues. Historical perspectives were leading. However, in the last decades, a wealth of material evidence was presented in studies on disability: amulets, archaeological excavation in temples with healing practices. This also regards the study of ancient inscriptions on tombs. Hence, Frits van der Meer was ahead of his days. In *Augustinus de Zielzorger,* he discussed many aspects of the day-to-day life of the bishop of Hippo in the context of archaeology and art history.

Likewise, patristic theology may profit from research in CSR. Etic perspectives probably offer additional knowledge which facilitates more in-depth analysis of theological concepts. Yet, it is vital that both disciplines respect each other. Some attempts have been made until yet. István Czachesz engaged with the function of the human body in his study *The Grotesque Body in Early Christian Discourse: Hell, Scatology and Metamorphosis* (2014). Among many other interesting issues, he discussed Pascal Boyer's theory of counter-intuitiveness. Yet, he aimed for an analysis in the context of the grotesque of the human body. Another thoughtful contribution was made by Troels Engberg-Pedersen. He is a known expert in Hellenism in Pauline thought. His contribution was added as epilogue to a volume on Judaism, early Christianity and cognitive and social sciences (Luomanen, P., Pyysiäinen, I., & Uro, R. [eds.], 2007, *Explaining Christian Origens and Early Judaism: Contributions from Cognitive and Social Science*). In a lucid reflection, Engberg-

Pedersen underlined opportunities for research in inclusion of relevant empirical data in patristic exegesis of theological ideas within historical contexts. However, he criticized CSR research for tendencies to reductionism. Much more serious was his complaint on widespread exclusion of reflection on theological ideas in CSR. Doctrine and theology are fundamental aspects of material evidence. Hence, publications lacking attention for this aspect of *Sitz im Leben* have a difficult task to convince a wider scholarly audience.

Let's try to raise some issues that may contribute to the understanding of Augustine's position in North African religious practice in etic perspective. First, Augustine was a bishop with both African and Roman roots. His biography shows his travels. The places where he lived successively are known. Particularly for his dialogues (AD 386–8), material artefacts such as the villa where the retreat in Cassiciacum was held offer promising sources. Thus, this well-documented example of Roman *otium* is studied better in the context of (material) early Christian culture. The place Cassiciacum has been identified as Cassago Brianza in the region of Lombardy. It has a rich archaeological history that goes back to the Neolithic period. It was possible to reach the place from Milan on the *Via Busa*. The latter was a known and well-maintained road with significant economic function. Thus, isolation in the Cassiciacum retreat implied a relatively mild form of solitude. Hence, not surprisingly, in Augustine's dialogues we can see the personages leaving and arriving at some points in the conversations. This malleable type of solitude fits well in the matter-of-fact function of *otium* in late-antique society. Solitude was voluntarily chosen. Good company of friends and a comfortable place that relieved participants from sorrows for maintenance of daily life helped to endure the hardships of life. Thus, time and energy for philosophical topics could be focussed again.

A supplementary aspect that might shine light on an etic perspective on Augustine's work is his preaching. Thousands of his sermons have survived. They present, often in the sideline, many details from the Christian community of, for example, Hippo or Carthago. In the recently discovered Dolbeau sermons, homily 20B sets off with Augustine making apologies for his absence because of illness. In the text, he reacted emotionally on the community which welcomed him with warm applause. The incident made evident that disease and recovery were experienced as social activities. Rituals, such as applause, marked reintegration in the community. Philological studies on the *Christus medicus*-metaphor in Augustine's sermons (Peter Eijkenboom) pointed out that Augustine was relatively well versed in antique sources on medicine. Though, medical metaphors functioned as explanations to spiritual healing. Particularly Paul's metaphor of milk for the little ones (*lac parvulorum*) was a favourite *topos*. Anthony Dupont came to a most important conclusion. He demonstrated that it was the context of liturgy that made Augustine select his arguments from a concrete Christian life. Hence, in sermons, many examples and metaphors started within the domain of direct experience in the faithful community (Dupont 2013, 626).

In the second chapter, I discussed Augustine's preference for sensible aspects in his expositions on Christology in *On Genesis against the Manicheans*. Close reading has revealed how Augustine protracted this preference for corporeality in pedagogical settings in the direction of sacramental theology. It was only later in his career, inspired by celebrations near the remains of the martyr St. Stephen in Uzalis, that he recognized miracles and healings around relics. Nevertheless, he warned his audience to be cautious and avoid mantic and amulets. Augustine's spiritual theology of healing referred to diseases that were well known to his audience. Like this, health problems functioned as examples in theology of martyrdom. Accordingly, bodily suffering enabled participation in Christ's wounds. In this manner, the crucifix operated as a corporeal sign. It became a sacrament for salvation from meaningless suffering.

Summarizing, an attempt for an etic perspective on Augustine reveals that many data are textual or related to some form of archaeological insight. Additionally, textual references to material aspects of daily life play their part in reconstructing an etic perspective on Augustine. This said, in the sections that follow now, I will return to the threefold Christological movement: kenosis, *Logos-Sarx* Christology and resurrection. In the following section on kenotic perspective, I discuss Augustine's kenotic view against the background of a small selection of Ilkka Pyysiäinen's work. Along these lines, I plan to review aspects from Augustine's theology with the assistance of types of argument in philosophy of religion, voiced by Pyysiäinen. Hereafter, renewed reading of *On Genesis against the Manicheans* facilitates us to discuss similarities between Augustine's kenosis and Pyysiäinen's ententional phenomena. In the second section of this chapter, it is my aim to return to Augustine's discussion of Platonists pride versus humility in *Confessions'* seventh book. Armin Geertz's embodied perspective on religion operates as a background. Thus, correspondences emerge between Armin Geertz theory on embodied religion and Augustine's preference for sensible examples in discourse. In the third section, resurrection is to be discussed with the help of *The City of God* XXII.14-17. Ilkka Pyysiäinen's discussion on teleological aspects of resurrection of the human body (Pyysiäinen 2015, 144) stipulated a contrasting view on Augustine's eschatological theology (Pyysiäinen 2003, 136–42).

4.3 Kenosis: Christ the God-man: A counter-intuitive agent?

The image of a self-emptying God has confirmed its vigorous power in theological reflection. In the previous chapters, we have seen that Augustine's texts voiced the vital function of kenotic exegesis in patristics. The biblical concept of a God, who is involved in history in the shape of a human being, urged him to carry out special theological strategies. In this manner, Paul's letter to the Philippians was as a scriptural benchmark that allowed patristic authors to reflect *in extenso* on this topic. Previously in this book, I argued that pastoral relevance can be found in healing sensemaking capacities. Along these lines, meaningless suffering possibly may be included within a process of deification. The metaphor of the *totus Christus* was Augustine's favourite to perform this pastoral task.

Kenotic theology goes well along with socially engaged religion. The perspective of liberation made a strong appeal on a temporarily vulnerable God possible. Accordingly, in nineteenth-century historical theology, a variety of kenotic theories emerged. These theories often operated with social models of Trinity. Eventually, scholars criticized radical kenotic theology for this reason. Particularly its tendency to widen the division between the divine Christ and his embodied shape was a target for criticism. Christ, in selective abstinence from exercise of powers, became the symbol of solidary with all who were forced to go without power and meaning. The sign of the cross thus became ambiguous. It refers to suffering, death as well as to resurrected health and perfection.

CSR has little to do with liberation movements. Cognitive sciences aim for methodological objectivity. Scholars from cognitive sciences appeal to natural explanations of religious phenomena. However, it has been noticed that CSR scholars have a strong interest in material, embodied aspects of religion. Hence, it seems relevant to compare Pyysiäinen's strategies to investigate embodied religion with Augustine's kenotic strategy. Yet, Augustine and Ilkka Pyysiäinen differ in many aspects. Firstly, their methods seem to contradict each other. Augustine is a biblical theist. Pyysiäinen focussed on objectivity in reason and method. Secondly, there is a huge distance over time. From the days of Augustine, a multitude of developments in science incited new debates. Nonetheless, the topic of the aspects of Augustine's kenotic theology is relevant in the context of types of argumentation in theist belief as mentioned by Pyysiäinen (Pyysiäinen 2015).

In his article, 'Theism Reconsidered: Belief in God and the Existence of God', Pyysiäinen contended against a simple dichotomy between theism and atheism. He argued that theist believers 'orient themselves toward a currently absent goal in ways that are described in the cognitive science of religion' (Pyysiäinen 2015, 147). As a consequence, religion is a natural phenomenon. However, Pyysiäinen analysed religion in terms of relationships with an absent transcendental entity. Maintaining these paradoxical relationships generates connectivity with a goal, a virtue or a motivation. Though, science and theology suffer from a homuncular concept of God. Since homuncular metaphors for God are in need for a first cause, they lead to infinite regression. Hence, Pyysiäinen argued that notions of absence and constraint in absential relationships will stop this need for causal regression. Pyysiäinen: 'Among absential relationships with real causal effects are functions, adaptations, thoughts, purposes, subjective experiences, and values' (Ibid. 146). Accordingly, in theistic belief, all relations are unfulfilled. They have been initiated by an absent Creator. In this way, Ilkka Pyysiäinen makes the impression to describe theist religion in terms of apophatic theory. 'The concept of God may be necessary for human freedom and value, but it acts as a placeholder for an absent actor that makes possible intentionality and ententional phenomena' (Ibid. 147).

While putting the finger on absence and constraint, a strong notion of kenosis developed. Hence, the second part of this section will be dedicated to a brief return to Augustine's kenotic exegesis in *On Genesis against the Manicheans* and *On Trinity*. The setting of this assessment is Pyysiäinen's exposé on ententional phenomena and relationships with absent essences. Though, to discuss this topic, a first task will be to sketch briefly Augustine's theological position in the context of types of argumentation discerned in philosophy of religion.

Types that were mentioned by Pyysiäinen are

- Theological realism versus nonrealism
- Rationality of belief
- Foundationalism versus nonfoundationalism
- Evidentialism versus nonevidentialism

In Chapter 3, I have sketched Augustine's philosophical position as a realist in search for rationality, *fides quaerens intellectum*. And yet, regarding the rationality of belief, Augustine did not see irrationality in biblical testimony. When confronted with scriptural texts that contradict or obscure, he suggested a hermeneutic of love (*On Christian Teaching*). Hence, language invites for deciphering in synergy with desire for wisdom. And so, the reader of the Bible may experience a variety of emotions: comfort as well as anxiety. God thus speaks within the process of reading. Otherwise, Augustine frequently proposed ideas and concepts from Neoplatonic and Stoic sources. Though, it was not evident for him to adopt their entire systems. Then again, the *Soliloquies* were written as internal dialogue. In this work, the personage Reason revealed human and divine attributes. Its prologue is full of Neoplatonic reminiscences. A concatenating ascent of predicates leads to ascension and aims for purification within the reader's mind. Henceforward (*Soliloquies* I.6.14), the metaphor of vision made Augustine spell out Neoplatonic notions of purification and union. *On the Happy Life*, which stems from the same period, shows strong affinity with Stoic ethics without rejecting Neoplatonic sources. These Stoic influences can be detected in Augustine's assessment of moderation.

About foundationalism, Augustine evidently held the position that faith needs a foundation. He had found it in the Bible and within apostolic tradition. And yet, Ilkka Pyysiäinen searched for a strictly rational foundation (Pyysiäinen 2015, 140). Firstly, Augustine is a biblical reasoner. Furthermore, in the words where Augustine spoke on relevance of the disciplines, it is obvious that he had an intense respect for reason. In this manner, eternal reason, present within the disciplines, makes it possible for humans to participate in divine Reason (*On Order*). Accordingly, in his dialogues Augustine was in search of rational foundation for what he was about to accept in faith as a neophyte. Progressive knowledge of the Bible and philosophy is reflected in Augustine's increasingly coherent exegesis of Genesis.

Was it necessary for Augustine to provide an explicit foundation for each detail in faith? This question is in need of different answers over changing periods in his life. The philosophical position that accepts multiple gradations in foundation was recently coined as relative foundationalism. Augustine's shift in belief may illustrate this phenomenon, as has been noticed by Anthony Dupont: Augustine's appreciation of healing miracles on the intercession of martyrs near relics of St. Stephen, later in his life. Otherwise, early in his career (*On the Happy Life),* Augustine expressed by means Monica's personage a firm belief in principle doctrines, such as Holy Trinity. As a result, for Augustine, a gradually deepening understanding in biblical foundation of the Nicene tradition of faith in the God-man Jesus Christ helped him discern which aspects of belief are most important, and which may eventually need future foundation.

From the perspective of evidentialism, Augustine did not hold that religion needs justification with naturalistic evidence. And yet, Augustine was not a clear-cut proponent of fideism. In anti-Pelagian works, he contended that nature was broken in Adamic sin. Nevertheless, creation continues to express the glory of God. In this manner, nature is the book of God. On the other side, it was obvious that theology was not just an academic language-game for Augustine. He was also a realist. Thus, he conceived signs that participate in Johannine hermeneutic theory of the words and of the Word. Particularly in-between these W/words, Augustine's ambiguity on language became apparent: signs and the thing itself. Language is a phenomenon in time. It is not of the same ontological status as its referent. Language enables humans along these lines to make a leap to immateriality. Its absent presence is a medium between humans and God. The Word, Christ, speaks within the language of Scripture. Augustine's arguments presuppose reasoning with and within the frames of biblical *topoi* and recurrent phrases. Speaking in terms of Pyysiäinen, Augustine's concept of human language was analogous to a *calculus,* a realistic *calculus.* Augustine told how he learned to speak and write in *Confessions* I.8.13–9.14. His account points out that, in his opinion, children learn by imitation and initiation. Hence, meaning is convention and operates within the nexus between human persons who agree on mutual goodwill to understand each other. God, the Word, is the One who can initiate speech in-between an ontological division that divides creation from Creator. He has spoken in Christ. He continues effective speech in the maintenance of cosmos and life. Hence, Christ was a universal hermeneutical key for Augustine.

Yet, Augustine situated the affective centre of God's speech in the mouth of the human Christ (Michael Cameron, 2012 *Christ Meets Me Everywhere. Augustine's Early Figurative Exegesis*). In fact, this process of communication parallels kenosis. According to Augustine, the speaking Word forbore its divine surplus while in temporal language. The sentences of the Bible speak the words of God. Though, they do not fully express meaning of God's Word. And so, on the topic of language, Augustine was not a radical universalist. Neither was he a radical conventionalist. Pragmatic aspects of conventions (intentions, beliefs and desires) reverberate in Ilkka Pyysiäinen's assessment of fideism. In fideism 'people believe in God because God is important for them (typically without explicit arguments)' (Pyysiäinen 2015, 141). Hence, religion is no fiction. In common sense, all varieties of inferences are made from religious concepts. 'However, the interesting thing is that the idea of God as an agent is at least compatible with all of them, and usually is explicitly presented as such. By this, I mean that God is supposed to have a mind in the sense of having intentions, beliefs and desires (although all his desires are by necessity fulfilled)' (Ibid. 141).

At first glance, Pyysiäinen's perspective reminds of the sceptic positions which Augustine discussed in *Contra Academicos*. However, in a broader sense, similarities with kenotic theological strategies come to the surface. In chapter 2, section 1.1.2, I contended that Augustine utilized the concept of a self-emptying God to counterbalance Johannine Christology of the Word (*GM* II.24.37; *Trin* II.5.8). Accordingly, in *On Genesis against the Manicheans*, Augustine argued that Gen. 2.24 referred not solely to human's departure from their parents. It was a metaphor for Christ the Word. He left his Father in incarnation. Henceforth, in the text, a kenotic turn was made. In quoting Phil. 2.7, he pointed out that incarnation did not involve any change within the nature of God. Therefore, I argued that Augustine's kenotic turn facilitated his assessment of unity between the three persons of Trinity.

On the other hand, Pyysiäinen's judgement of the concept of God shows relativistic features: 'For a cognitive scientist of religion, and for empirical study of religion in general, it does not really matter which of these philosophical views is most plausible or truth-like' (Pyysiäinen 2015, 141). Apparently, Augustine's realism directed to a different position. Yet, Ilkka Pyysiäinen's evaluation of ententional relationships (absent essences) uncovered functional parallels with Augustine's kenotic Christology. Absence and constraint were keywords in Pyysiäinen's discourse. Augustine explained a self-emptying God: He who forbore *and* revealed the divine Father. Hence, Augustine pointed out how cosseting our weaknesses signified the intense relationship between the Father and the Son.

Ententional relationships have constraint and absence as major attributes. For this reason, Pyysiäinen quoted Terence Deacons (2012): the 'neologism ententional is a generic adjective that describes all phenomena that are intrinsically incomplete "in the sense of being in relationship to, constituted by, or organized to achieve something nonintrinsic," that is, phenomena that are recognized for what they are by virtue of a goal or an end that is physically and energetically absent' (Pyysiäinen 2015, 144).

In this fashion, Pyysiäinen moved on towards negative theology. He approached religion with a negative epistemology: on what is not (yet) known. For Augustine, the reverse position is dominant. The sphere of influence of religion is everywhere and in everything. God the Creator and God who emptied himself of certain powers were the same person. Hence, we learned in the previous chapters that a kenotic perspective made it possible for him to link contrasting perspectives of omnipotence and embodied existence. All the same, Augustine's strategy was not to limit space for religion. On the contrary, he expanded it to that what has not yet been in existence. The fragment of *On Genesis against the Manicheans* II.24.37 revealed that it was Augustine's purpose to employ prophetic perspective in comments on the book of Genesis. For this reason, Adam's broken condition was contrasted to the stature of Christ. Paul's letter to the Philippians provided him with scriptural footage for this type of prophetic exegesis. Hence, special attention for sensible and corporeal aspects within the process of salvation supported him to join the divine Word, as well as embodied attributes of Jesus (kenosis) in his explanations of the book of Genesis.

CHRISTOLOGY IN DIALOGUE   105

Ilkka Pyysiäinen leaves some space for theism. Though, it is kenotic theism.

Thus, theistically interpreted human existence is ententional as it is 'being in relationship' to a physically and energetically absent God. This kind of absence is not the same thing as proven nonexistence, however. The 'pull' of the future possibility of 'being with God' lacks materiality, except for the real cognitive-emotional processes in which this 'pull' is realized. These are not merely something individual, but become cultural when shared by a large number of people for a long enough period of time. (Pyysiäinen 2015, 148)

Pyysiäinen sketched a subtle diagnostic picture. He described division between atheism and theism as a grey zone. In this fashion, he allowed many shades and open spaces. Augustine was more distinct in his days. Possibly, he would have correlated this type of argument with sceptic wisdom. In *Against the Academics,* he contended that sceptic wisdom had showed itself as exoteric, pragmatical presentation of esoteric Platonic wisdom (*Against the Academics* III.37–38). Augustine's perspective on incarnation was more inclusive (*Trin* II.5.8). In the previous chapters, it was mentioned that Augustine commented on incarnation: the Son was sent in what already was his own. Hence, that Christ was born 'from the virgin Mary' did not refer to a supernatural trick. Accordingly, Augustine gave precedence to embodied qualities of incarnation. Moreover, material reality was evaluated in a positive manner in contrast to Manicheans' perception. Within the human body, humankind was not only wounded but also healed. 'Therefore, in that He was born of God, He was in the world; but in that He was born of Mary, He was sent and came into the world' (*Trin* II.5.8). Hence, science and reason were not in contradiction with theism. Apparently, the story of creation as voiced within the book of Genesis, and Augustine's subsequent doctrinal reflection linked reason with theistic cosmology. However, religious perspectives add to, and do not necessarily deny or contradict, naturalistic claims. Nevertheless, reductionism sometimes was an uninvited consequence of perspectives. Thus, sometimes reductionism fulfilled its own prophecies. Dialogue, or attempts for colloquial conversation, may direct debate in philosophical theology to new horizons.

Personal reflection

God's omnipotence, omniscience and omnipresence improve safe havens for all what is weak, stupid and narrow-minded within society. Though, what is more powerful, more wise and more existent than I can conceive is not necessarily God. Even an augmentation may operate as a reduction. God is not a commander in absence. God is not an extension of human power, knowledge or existence. Augustine appreciated positive theology, as well as negative theology. Both routes apart from each other head towards separation. It will lead the perplexed of our century astray. Moving between both tracks leads to doubt. Doubt to speak or to remain silent? Is this apophatic theology?

Negative theology does not remain silent. It speaks on God's absence in many words. Apophatic theology needs confidence to be effective. Is ineffability a form of confidence? In its negativity, yes. Though, no predicate expresses fully what it's meant to say. Is this a reason to convert to agnosticism? Not to know God fully is a normal situation, while confronted with an omnipotent, omniscient and omnipresent essence. Knowing everything would make equal to God: whatever, wherever and Who-ever. Hence, all knowledge in words, signs or images speak in apophasis.

4.4 Augustine and embodied anthropology: The Word in a body?

Between Chalcedonian *Logos-Sarx* Christology and contemporary embodied anthropology gapes a division. Furthermore, Western society's individualism gives the impression to be at odds with universalistic claims of *Logos-Sarx* Christology. Hence, not surprisingly, Augustine's Christology frequently was epitomized as Johannine and Logos-centred. However, in the previous sections we have seen that kenotic theology Augustine lends a hand, to link up day-to-day existence of a North African Christian community with an overarching concept of a healing in the *totus Christus*.

Despite these healing capacities, comments were made on Augustine's voluntarism. With benefit from Marilyn McCord Adam's horror-defeating model, I discussed this topic in Chapter 3. In the next section, it is my intention to talk over Augustine's assessment of humility versus Platonic pride in *Confessions* VII, in dialogue with Armin Geertz's plea for embodied anthropology.

Obviously, Augustine didn't know about MRI scanners. He knew nothing of neurobiological insights on the 'hardware' of the brain. Nevertheless, it is suggestive that Augustine throughout his preaching work preferred examples from the day-by-day life of his audience. More often, these *exempla* were corporeal, or referred to biblical persons or topics. Armin Geertz's contention that insights from neurobiology are to be included in research on religion makes it relevant to return to Augustine's preference for examples from the domain of the senses. Geertz argued that especially these objects have a crucial function in the transmission and development of religion: religious people do ascribe supernatural attributes to these objects. Hence, it seems that Augustine's preference for examples from sensible domain finds corroboration in Geertz's research on embodied religious practice.

For that reason, it is my aim now to address briefly some major characteristics of Armin Geertz's embodied anthropology. After that, there will be a good moment to return towards Augustine's fragment on Platonic pride. The humility of the embodied Christ is Augustine's track (Christification) and goal (resurrection). This said, I want to return to Armin Geertz's appeal for embodied study of religion.

Armin Geertz was active in CSR from the very beginning. Thus, he was able to gain profit from parallel progressions made in neurosciences. From the debate that emerged, it became obvious that research on religion no longer should leave contributions from neurology aside. Hence, Geertz made efforts to study groundbreaking work from the Portuguese neuroscientist Antonio Damasio. With MRI-scans, Damasio was able to match regions within the physical brain with activities. He even detected areas that were already active, before a conscious decision has been made. Hence, Damasio assessed conscious brain activity as a product of physical processes in the brain. However, research on evolutionary brain-development has clarified how functional modules have evolved in time. Subsequent theories valued religion for its function within social cohesion. And so, religion was studied as a cultural phenomenon within sociology and anthropology. In his reaction, Armin Geertz intended to discern which characteristics and mechanisms religions as systems share. Supernatural agents, physical objects and religious practice were important concepts in the publications that followed.

In Armin Geertz's contributions of books on methods in CSR, his efforts were directed to open traditional theology for insights from his discipline. More than Ilkka Pyysiäinen, it seems, Armin Geertz left space to discuss exclusive functions of religion. All the same, systems of religion are in his view basically neurobiological and embodied. Neurological circuits facilitate the transmission of different types of knowledge. Still, Armin Geertz contended that religion is a product of natural human capacities. However, emergent interpersonal knowledge in religious systems in this view includes universal wisdom and common consciousness. In this fashion, sacred spaces and embodied rituals have a crucial function in cultural transmission in evolution.

In his chapter on methods in CSR in *Cognitive Approaches to the Study of Religion*, Armin Geertz states:

> The main point of this chapter is simple: there is more to cognitive theory than hitherto assumed in the comparative study of religion. Possibilities for future research are enormous. All that is required, on the one hand, is humility in the face of a sea of information and a plurality of epistemologies, and, on the other, creative application on one of humanity's most evocative and encompassing inventions. Indeed, if we succeed in understanding the most fundamental aspects of human cognition (consciousness, representation, symbolization, language, and emotion), I am convinced that we will discover how crucial a role religious ritual and religious ideas have played in making us what we are. (Geertz 2004, 385)

Humility as a track in the study of religion. Material objects, examples taken from daily life, and illnesses operated as metaphors for humanity's spiritual defectiveness. Augustine's theology revealed many coincidences of representations, symbolization, words and emotions. The wealth in forms and arguments in the study of religion is awesome and provokes humility. Yet, in theological research data from CSR have not been used widely so far. A fine specimen of a cross-over project is Armin Geertz's recently initiated research on texts of Theresa of Avila. He mined her texts on reported religious experiences, techniques and activities. His purpose was to achieve insights in interaction between bodily actions and religious thinking. His experience in research on cultural embeddedness of human cognition made Armin Geertz ready for this project.

Before we take some time to address some aspects of Geertz's embodied anthropology, there is a subtlety that should be mentioned. Armin Geertz never simply reduced religion to physical brain activity. His statement:

> Culture and social relations and institutions are back again, centre stage, in the story of cognition. Cognition is not just about the brain. It is more precisely and more correctly about *interacting* brains. It is about brains that cannot even use their highly evolved capacities without supportive cultural symbolic systems – language for one thing, but also the myriads of other cultural systems, among them religious symbolic systems. (Geertz 2008, 8)

Accordingly, he concluded that religious practices between interacting brains emerge from physical processes but are not necessarily reduced to physical processes.

Now it is time to focus on Armin Geertz's conception of interacting levels in embodied religion. In his defence for a biocultural theory of religion, Armin Geertz suggested that every theory of religion should focus on five aspects: origen, form, function, structure and meaning. Each of these aspects requires analysis on four levels: neurobiology, cognitive psychology, sociology and lastly a semantic-semiotic level (Geertz 2010, 315). Geertz pinpointed the function of religion on the level of cultural systems. Though, he acknowledged that religion is about interaction between material objects and their symbolic functions. Hence, not surprisingly, religions are emergent systems that come to the fore in biology. Thus, 'we need to pay more attention to the neurobiology of religion and culture. We are, as argued, not just mental creatures, but, perhaps even more so, somatic creatures. When confronted with religious claims and behaviours, we must not only think of the semantic, sociological and psychological aspects but also the neurological and somatic aspects' (Geertz 2010, 314). In a summarizing table, Armin Geertz mentioned material symbols and material culture in semantic-semiotic and sociological levels. So, we can learn from Armin Geertz that whoever studies religious language (texts) and ritual ought to pay attention for its embodied context. It is in this context that Augustine's preference for examples from day-to-day life in sermons and in the Cassiciacum dialogues is relevant.

Additionally, Geertz assessed worldviews as structures that process knowledge on the level of semantic and semiotics. And yet, they are anchored in cognitive networks (psychology) and brain (neurobiological level). Hence, religion incorporates semantic and semiotic functions (texts) in cognitive-emotional effects (ritual, sacraments). Accordingly, Augustine's preference for 'at-hand' examples shows similarities to Geertz's contentions. Though, at the pulpit, doctrinal content was often not prior in chronology for Augustine. His sermons were exemplary for this principle. Usually, as a first step, audiences' attention was caught with the assistance of 'at-hand' examples. From that moment, Augustine linked emotional appeal with biblical or theological content. In this fashion, he directed his audience in pastoral and doctrinal reflection. As a result, liturgy and sacred space shaped the way religion functioned in embodied context. Armin Geertz was interested in structures of religion. Together with Jeppe Sinding Jensen, he described the activity of religions: they 'formalize systems of knowledge into schemata which serve as meaningful frameworks for action and knowledge' (Jensen 2003, 125; Geertz 2010, 316).

Most abstract is the modus in which religion functions on neurological level. Geertz described this type of activity as 'a broader brain culture interface'. It effectuates interaction and communication between processes. Armin Geertz endeavoured to address the crucial role of 'material and non-material tools and gadgets that connect mind, brain and body in systematic ways' (Geertz 2010, 316). As an illustration, I intend to read again Augustine's plead for humility while confronted with Platonic pride. Augustine pointed out that humility functions as a track that starts in corporeal reality and leads to a new situation. Thus, Augustine empowered his audiences' capacity to recognize divine presence within material existence. Hence, embodied religion initiates deification through inclusion of non-optimal conditions of life within a vision of liberation.

At this point, I will return to Augustine's *Logos-Sarx* Christology. As previous readings have revealed, in Augustine's account on Platonic pride versus humility in Christ (*Confessions* VII), the theological topic of incarnation is prevalent. Consequentially, humans start their trails towards freedom on the side of trajectory signs and sensible things: body, objects and symbols. Thus, humility granted Augustine with the insight that the name of Christ became the Word that, when received, gave the 'power to become the sons of God, as many as believed in His name' (*Conf* VII.9.13).

> And Thou, willing first to show me how Thou resistest the proud, but givest grace unto the humble, and by how great an act of Thy mercy Thou hadst traced out to men the way of humility, in that Thy Word was made flesh, and dwelt among men: Thou procuredst for me, by means of one puffed up with most unnatural pride, certain books of the Platonists, translated from Greek into Latin. And therein I read, not indeed in the very words, but to the very same purpose, enforced by many and divers reasons, that In the beginning was the Word, and the Word was with God, and the Word was God: the Same was in the beginning with God: all things were made by Him, and without Him was nothing made: that which was made by Him is life, and the life was the light of men, and the light shineth in the darkness, and the darkness comprehended it not. And that the soul of man, though it bears witness to the light, yet itself is not that light; but the Word of God, being God, is that true light that lighteth every man that cometh into the world. And that He was in the world, and the world was made by Him, and the world knew Him not. But, that He came unto His own, and His own received Him not; but as many as received Him, to them gave He power to become the sons of God, as many as believed in His name; this I read not there. (*Conf* VII.9.13, transl. Pusey)

Augustine did not simply regret omission; he was unhappy about Platonists' pride. In incarnation, it was endorsed that creation participated in God's universal plan of salvation. Hence, even in a fallen state, creatures reflect their origen. Accordingly, Augustine included vulnerable, embodied life within redemption. Thus, not surprisingly, the track of humility is not a flight in transcendence. It is an immanent path of embodied religious life. Consequently, Augustine's perspective of humility incorporated human weakness within the *totus Christus*.

Revisiting Geertz's request not to ignore insights from neurobiological level within study of religion, the question of how this biological level relates to patristic research on Augustine comes again into view. Earlier in this book, it was mentioned that Augustine was relatively well informed in medicine. However, the idea of physical structures shaping religious experience not self-evidently agrees with Augustine's concept of religion. Though, he did not exclude completely the relevance of physical processes. The track of humility provided him with access to the realm of corporeal objects in religion.

Humility involves willingness to scrutinize older concepts. It opens receptiveness for new comprehensions within dialogue. Augustine received new ideas not without critical evaluation. Though, he preferred to start inquiry within his immediate environment. He avoided arguments presupposing knowledge from esoteric sources. Are insights from neuroscience esoteric? Not for those who have access and are able to understand. Yet, a majority of Augustine's intended audience ask for other sources. New dialogue is required.

Otherwise, Augustine did not avoid complex reasonings. Regularly, his texts presuppose skills in philosophical reasoning. In this fashion, he drew attention to the *libri platonicorum*. Thus, he praised authors for deep insights but criticized them for pride. Hence, he recommended humility as a recognition of the itinerary in incarnation. And so, Augustine utilized medical concepts as metaphors for spiritual development and growth. This strategy fits in Augustine's category of use and instruments (*uti/frui*). Moreover, Augustine most likely would have welcomed these disciplines, as they are useful to understand the Word of God. For now, theology is invited to react on the invitation to proceed on the track of humility: participation in the study of embodied religion. Vice versa, for CSR scholars patristic theology presents new opportunities to include reflection on theological ideas in their research.

Personal reflection

Theology from its very nature asks for humility. Theology aims to make sense of religious belief. It explains complex interactions between lived practice and doctrinal reflection. Theology cannot but turn to humility in the face of reflection on what has been called 'God' or 'god' or 'something'. Even 'something' transcends my capacity to understand in detail what is going on in day-by-day life. A fortiori, God goes far beyond the comprehension of what can be understood.

Even though ritual and words are my daily food, I highly esteem what scholars have achieved. That academic study, based on naturalistic methods improves our understanding of religion, is not a topic that is disputed. For this reason, I see it adds a new dimension. By nature, it does not explain ultimately. Theology wishes to reflect on ultimate questions. It asks for humility, seeing what human reason has achieved.

4.5 The risen body: Absent presence?

The idea of resurrection after death voiced an overarching ideal of eternal life and restoration. And yet, what can be thought of this dream in the age that biology is in search of mechanisms and functions? Before Augustine, it was Aristotle who pronounced teleology in what he observed in nature. Everything that is strives towards a goal that is appropriate to its essence. Hence, movements continually change the conditions of life. Adaptation to a new equilibrium is required. The good is in-between. While external circumstances change, the centre changes.

In the first paragraph of this chapter, I underlined that Ilkka Pyysiäinen's approach to religion shows tensions as well as similarities with Augustine's kenotic Christology. Resemblances particularly involved Augustine's *and* Pyysiäinen's drive to spell out the phenomenon of religion with the help of supernatural agents in a non-optimal world. Ilkka Pyysiäinen recommended to leave the homuncular concept of God aside. Constraint and absence replaced this concept of God (Pyysiäinen 2015, 146–7). Consequentially, tensions became apparent with Augustine's Christ-centred theology. On the other hand, Augustine's cautious formulations evoked apophatic theology. Pyysiäinen's critique on homuncular God concepts in theology as well as in science urged to appreciate negative and absent relationships. Thus, we have seen, he avoided the need for a first cause, and solved infinite regress that threatens anthropomorphic concepts of God. Pyysiäinen states:

> Like the homunculus, God in all His greatness is a mysterious agent responsible for consciousness, intelligence, and the apparent order in the world. I call 'homuncular' all arguments that explain mind, self-hood, and even the ordered universe by postulating an unobservable intelligent agent as the ultimate source and basis of these phenomena. Such explanation, however, leads to an infinite regress because the homunculus-God itself calls for an explanation. (Pyysiäinen 2015, 143)

Hence, tensions between positive and negative epistemological aspects of Pyysiäinen's theory of religion came into sight. On the one, positive, side, he investigated behaviour and spread of counter-intuitive attributes to objects from daily life in religion. On the other side, Pyysiäinen underlined negative epistemology in the functions he ascribed to relationships with absent essences. Elsewhere, he argued that 'the emergence of Christianity thus cannot be explained without explaining why and how the relevant beliefs were successful in cultural selection; this, in turn, presupposes other arguments in addition to the idea of visions or hallucinations' (Pyysiäinen 2007, 61).

In the final book of *The City of God*, a similar ambiguity can be detected (*CG* XXII.14-17). On the one hand, Augustine described similarities between the temporal human body and a resurrected body. These resemblances allow the same person to maintain identity in a resurrected body. However, the body is going to be healed. Weaknesses and diseases will be disappeared. Along these lines, it is a spiritual body in perfection. On the other hand, there is Augustine's Christology. It asserts truly embodied existence of Jesus as the Saviour. Hence, Augustine's interest in a positive assessment of the human body within the person of Christ was talked over in reference to Paul's kenotic theology. Moreover, maintaining Johannine *Logos-Sarx* oriented Christology within his theory of Trinity, in juxtaposition with kenotic assessment of incarnation, was not difficult for Augustine.

Until yet, we have focussed on Augustine's idea of resurrection and Pyysiäinen's comments on homuncular concepts of God. This said, it is the moment to take some more time to look at the combination of Augustine's ideas on the resurrected body, Ilkka Pyysiäinen's assessment of folk psychology, and his picture of constraint relationships with absent essences.

In the conclusion of his contribution in *Zygon*, Ilkka Pyysiäinen summarized that popular belief, folk psychology and CSR not necessarily exclude each other. 'In folk psychology, God may still be understood in a homuncular sense, but the concept can be explained in a nonhomuncular way by reverse engineering human mind and its evolution, although this does not reveal any specific point in the emergent processes where "God" suddenly comes up' (Pyysiäinen 2015, 147–8). In Augustine's position as a bishop, pastoral practicalities urged him to deal with folk psychology. As a writing theologian, he dealt with explanations on God in a nonhomuncular way, particularly in his reflections on Holy Trinity. Obviously, Augustine was conscious of God's ineffability. Hence, theology's incapacity to utter God's perfection fully was familiar to him. Though, as previous readings in this book have shown, he was not reluctant to elaborate on the risen body and its age. Augustine states:

> We are left, therefore, with one conclusion, namely, that each of us will have that size we had in our maturity, even though we die in extreme old age; or we shall have that size we would have had in our maturity, in case we died earlier. Hence, we must interpret St. Paul's words concerning 'the mature measure of the fullness of Christ' as meaning, for example, that the measure of His fullness will be reached when all of His members, the Christian people, will have been added to Christ the Head; or the words may mean, if they have reference to the resurrection, that all will rise with bodies neither less nor larger than the size of their mature age, and so in the age and vigour of thirty years-since that is the age reached by Christ and the age which even secular authorities consider the age of mature manhood and the age beyond which a man declines toward the weakness of old age. That is why St. Paul did not speak of the measure either of the body or of the stature but of 'the measure of the age of the fullness of Christ'. (*CG* XXII.15)

Evidently, in this text Augustine outlined a homuncular concept of embodied resurrection. However, he underlined absent aspects of the human person in resurrection (marriage, lust) as well. These absences prompted ententional relationships. '[T]he measure of His fullness *will* be reached when all of His members, the Christian people, *will have been added* to Christ the Head' (*CG* XXII.15). Augustine's expressions in future tense denoted absence and 'not yet', until all has been accomplished. Accordingly, Augustine's Christological theory of eschatology urged him to utilize embodied language. Consequently, absence and constraint were justified in future completion.

Otherwise, Augustine's narrative on the risen body is a fine example of attribution of counter-intuitive features to a corporeal entity: the human body. Ilkka Pyysiäinen states:

> As I see it, quite irrespective of whether or not all such ideas have had survival value for the species, the capacity for agent detection has been an evolutionary advantage. Postulating the existence of counter-intuitive agents may merely be parasitic on this ability and the ability to form cross-domain representations (See Pyysiäinen 2001b). This in turn means that, besides the perceived natural environment, the conceptual reality constructed by humans is also always partly ambiguous and contains slots that people are tempted to fill by representations of counter-intuitive agents. (Pyysiäinen 2003, 68)

Certainly, Augustine's perspective on the human body is ambiguous. So is his view on the person of Christ. Hence, Augustine filled it in as a representation of *the* counter-intuitive agent. He made Christ an icon. An invisible God, visible in time and matter. Thus, Pyysiäinen seemed to be correct when he argued that the researchers' perspective on creation determines the concept of God. Whenever God is conceived as a Creator, the concept of a homuncular God looms. 'I shall argue that these kinds of ideas of God as the Creator follow a similar logic as attempts to explain human consciousness and intentionality by postulating another agent, a homunculus, inside an individual' (Pyysiäinen 2015, 142).

Towards the end of book XXII of *The City of God*, Augustine mentioned other absent aspects of the life of the risen person:

> For myself, I think that those others are more sensible who have no doubt that both sexes will remain in the resurrection. After all, there will then be none of that lust which is the cause of shame

in connection with sex, and so, all will be as before the first sin, when the man and the woman were naked and felt no shame. In the resurrection, the blemishes of the body will be gone, but the nature of the body will remain. (*CG* XXII.17)

And so, defects, lust and shame will have disappeared. Marriage will have been vanished. 'In the resurrection, then, there will be those who on earth "marry" and those who "are given in marriage". Only, in heaven there will be no marriage' (*CG* XXII.17). In the previous sections of this book, I suggested that, on the topic of the risen body, embodiment was partially described in what it is not. 'And, in this sense, the test refers to the resurrection of our bodies. However, we must remember that, even in this interpretation, the "conformity" is no more a matter of the size of our bodies in the resurrection than the "measure" in the other text refers to size. It is a matter of maturity' (*CG* XXII.15).

Augustine thus carried out positive as well as negative theology. Not many theologians typified Augustine as an apophatic theologian. Paul van Geest (*The Incomprehensibility of God: Augustine as a negative theologian*, 2011) discussed apophatic qualities of Augustine's theology. Many of these features found their origen in the so-called anti-Pelagian polemic. Accordingly, Augustine was able to discuss God's grace in correspondence with weakened human capacities. Hence, another example of Augustine references to affective relationships with absent essence.

Personal reflection

Resurrection and healing offer comfort. A homuncular God is close and near-by. But is it real? Certainly, humans believe in God because, in their opinion, it is good for them to do so. Science investigates what is real. Pyysiäinen and Augustine both contended goodness of constraint relationships with absence. Thus, space for desire has been created. It is now more than ever urgent to investigate desire. How do they work out in our world? CSR offers a wealth of information and insights. Though, it adds, and does not eradicate. Hence, tolerance, dialogue and cooperation will help.

Why should a theologian decide to study CSR? The more opinions, the more interactions? The more interaction, the more relationships of working brains? My respect for Augustine as a theologian is great. My respect for what a community achieves in prayer – relationship in absence and constraint – is huge. My respect for both prayer and argumentative thought is immense. Thoughts on God or absence of God are welcome. God may see what true or defective thought is. What is reason? Who is God?

4.6 Conclusion

The challenge to incorporate insights from evolutionary biology, cognitive sciences and theology would have been a major experiment for Augustine. Nonetheless, in the previous chapter we have seen that, despite his anti-bodily reputation, Augustine concurred that embodied perspectives have relevance. The three scholars, Augustine, Armin Geertz and Ilkka Pyysiäinen, were somehow involved with research on religious practice in its day-to-day context. Above all, readings in preceding sections confirmed that Augustine's pedagogy started within and on corporeal level: *per corpora ad incorporalia*. In his doctrinal reflection, Augustine was a realist. He accepted the authority of the Bible and doctrinal declarations made on the council of Nicaea. Thus, his perspective on world and humankind is a theist view. He accepted the concept of an incarnated God who created cosmos. Hence, Ilkka Pyysiäinen would characterize Augustine's concept of God as homuncular.

In the first paragraph, I discussed Ilkka Pyysiäinen's proposal to set aside homuncular concepts of God in the context of Augustine's kenotic theology in *On Genesis against the Manicheans*. Both authors focussed on absence and constraint. And yet, Augustine preferred a Christological anthropology. Hence, he justified embodied participation in perfection of deficiencies. Thus, non-optimal human conditions were included within a framework of healing and eschatological perfection. Hence, tensions as well as functional similarities became apparent in Augustine's theology and Ilkka Pyysiäinen's approach. Some of these dissimilarities and similarities have been noticed in the first section of this chapter. Tensions came into sight while Pyysiäinen argued for a non-homuncular concept of God, and Augustine concurred a Christological account of incarnation and creation. Still, unity within the person of Christ and within Trinity was normative for Augustine. Effectively, the combination of homuncular theology and kenosis made Augustine capable to cope with the burdens of daily life in early Christian community. Though, Pyysiäinen's *desideratum* to replace the homuncular concept of God for constraint and relationships with absent divine agencies was partly fulfilled in Augustine's kenotic embodied Christology. Then, Augustine gave language a very special position in his theology. That's why the Christ-Logos was able to speak and act within the division between creation and Creator. Hence, it was remarked that Ilkka Pyysiäinen's critical assessment of the homuncular concept of God exposes methodological similarities with Augustine's discussion with scepticism. Pyysiäinen as well as late-antique academic scepticism argued for minimalist epistemology: they wish 'to stay safe'.

In the second section of this chapter, I re-examined Augustine's account on Platonic pride *(Confessions VII)* in juxtaposition with Armin Geertz's embodied anthropology. All over his oeuvre, Geertz emphasized relevance of neurobiology for the study of religious practice. Given that religion functions as a brain-culture interface, it initiates interaction and communication between neural and cultural processes. Hence, religion as systems, and in religious practices, material and non-material tools and gadgets link mind, brain and body. As a result, I suggested that Augustine's preference for material and sensible *exampla* in preaching and pedagogy shows methodological parallels with Armin Geertz's wish for embodied and even embrained anthropology. For Augustine, acknowledgement of sensible and corporeal objects initiating theological reflection (incarnation) was a first step on the track of humility. Yet, use *(uti)* of corporeal objects was instrumental for spiritual growth. Thus, with Armin Geertz's admonition in mind, Augustine's exhortation on humility may imply for CSR scholars an opportunity to include patristic texts in their research. Hence, developments and praxis of early Christian religious life may be clarified with the assistance of reflection on the theological ideas involved. And the other way around: theology and patristic researchers are invited to respect and study insights from embodied study of religion, neurobiological science and cognitive sciences.

The third section of this chapter was dedicated to resurrection and to Ilkka Pyysiäinen's suggestion to replace homuncular concepts of God. We have read his considerations on this topic in discussion with Augustine's idea on the risen body in *The City of God,* book XXII. The resurrected body will live in size and maturity of the risen Christ. Even though this view on resurrection apparently is homuncular, I contended that Augustine's Christological assessment of heavenly perfection within resurrection urged him to use embodied language in a positive manner. However, conceptual attributes never express all details of reality. The use of them denotes absence and constraint in the relationship between a believer and the eschatological goal. Thus, we can conclude that homuncular theology did not withheld Augustine to put a combination of positive theology and apophatic argument into operation.

Now that we have made for the third time the threefold movement from kenosis to *Logos-Sarx* Christology towards the resurrection, it has become clear that insights from the study of patristics, CSR and biology do not match in an easy manner. They require a dialogue with respect for identity of each of the disciplines. Though, re-evaluation of selected fragments from Augustine's oeuvre in the context of a selection of ideas from CSR scholars, Armin Geertz and Ilkka Pyysiäinen, revealed that there are at least functional parallels. Moreover, the three scholars have their fascination for the phenomenon of religion in common. They share a strong motivation to understand religion and faith in a rational manner: *fides quaerens intellectum.*

And yet, for Augustine, the template for investigation of religion in a rational manner included reflection on belief in a non-material God-person. For both CSR scholars, Armin Geertz and Ilkka Pyysiäinen, the paradigm for their inquiries on religion were dominated by the requirement of evidence-based methods in empirical research. Thus, there are major differences between Augustine's theology and research on religion in the twenty-first century. Though, as we have seen, the three perspectives reveal powerful insights into the phenomenon of religion.

Are they able to complement each other? No, when it comes to a confrontation between Augustine's knowledge on medical science and contemporary neurobiological research on hardware of the human brain. Yes, when it comes to a functional analysis of what Augustine and CSR scholars aimed for in their investigations on religion. Therefore, I suggest including the format of dialogue within the discipline of philosophical theology. Augustine's choice for dialogue did not end with his decision to abandon the literary genre. He continued epistolary dialogue and was in his theological treatises in a continuing conversation with proponents and adversaries. In method, there is work to do. An interdisciplinary approach that puts a combination of hermeneutical analysis and analytic tools from recent philosophy into operation is not self-evident. Yet, it is my conviction that imperfection should not lead immediately to the conclusion of impossibility. Philosophers *and* theologians are experienced researchers on imperfection. Philosophical theology hence requires reflection *and* interaction.

Scholars in twenty-first-century patristic theology have recognized the relevance of topics such as religious violence, gender, orthodoxy and heterodoxy. They contributed to a more complete picture of early Christian era. Despite distance in time between Augustine's texts, Armin Geertz and Ilkka Pyysiäinen, in their turn, did contribute to the understanding of early Christian religion. Augustine's written works that were filtered through his intellect and faith reveal insights on early Christian religion. In this perspective, his oeuvre offers a wealth of data and insights on the package of lived faith. Evidentially, there is a huge amount of raw material for textual fieldwork for CSR scholars in early Christianity. And, vice versa, there is a huge amount of insights on the phenomenon of religion, provided by cognitive sciences on religion. They invite patristic scholars to have a fresh look at religious practice in early Christianity.

.

5

Conclusion

At the end of this book, a tour and some detours have been made. However, many details have been left unattended. The title suggested topics focussing on the person of Christ from a relative wide angle of disciplines. The human body, in its vulnerability, has been placed in the centre. Divine attributes such as omnipotence and perfection have been discussed within a theological perspective on the embodied Jesus of Nazareth. He has been identified as the Christ within the Holy Trinity.

A lot of expectations were expressed at the beginning of the book. There has been a desire that re-reading Augustine would provide the discussion between dualism and physicalism with 'relevant ideas and perspectives' (Chapter 1). Moreover, a wish for 'renewed speech on unity and the human body' (Chapter 2) and the desire for a dialogue of hospitality was expressed in the introductory sections of this book. New speech? Hardly! Renewed speech? Yes, but on the shoulders of giants in scholarship! Dialogue of hospitality? Yes, I think so. Let's have another brief look on it.

In the first chapter, I briefly introduced philosophical and patristic aspects of the concept of unity. Christ was a leading example. Because reflection on Jesus the Christ in systematic theology was centred on at least three branches, I have chosen to stick to this threefold movement throughout this book: kenosis, *Logos-Sarx* Christology and the risen Christ. This movement represents for me personally overarching dynamics of creation, incarnation, salvation and perfection.

The second chapter was devoted to facets of Augustine's assessment of the human body within these perspectives. Selected fragments from his written work *(On Genesis against the*

Manicheans, *On Trinity*, *Confessions* and *The City of God)* were our benchmarks. The metaphor of a kenotic self-emptying God was discussed from the angle of Manichaean criticism. Genesis' account on the paradise lost and God's response in adaptation to humankind's weakness offered Augustine scriptural materials to repudiate Manichean criticism. Augustine's theology of mediation in wounded love had found full expression in major works, such as *On Trinity*. A second perspective of *Logos-Sarx* Christology was illuminated with the assistance of a fragment from his *Confessions*. In this paragraph from the seventh book, Augustine deliberated on his impression of Platonic books in contrast with a track of humility in God's incarnation in the person of Christ. The third section of Chapter 2, on Augustine, focussed on the perspective of unity in perfection with the help of a fragment of the closing book of *The City of God*. Albeit detailed in its speculation on the risen human body, Augustine's theology of the resurrected body remained ambiguous. The human body will be perfected, but according to the ideal state of humanly measures: the risen body of Christ.

With these insights from Augustine as a point of departure, I have focussed on creation, incarnation and the human body in Chapter 3. Instead of patristic reflection, this chapter had philosophical theology as its dominating point of view. After a brief orientation on the discipline of philosophical theology, we have returned to the fragments of Augustine's work from Chapter 2. Thus, the Christological perspectives kenosis, Logos and resurrection came up again. Yet, in this chapter Augustine's deliberations were talked over in dialogue with Marilyn McCord Adams theodicy (horror-defeating), Thomas Morris' two-mind model in Christology and Trenton Merricks' physicalist picture of the resurrected body. The result of this attempt to dialogue was that, despite tensions and dissimilarities, common ground was found in a shared goal: exploration on the fascinating idea of divine action in human shape.

In Chapter 4, the step was made towards CSR. Again, the fragments from Augustine's written work asked for attention. This time, they were read in dialogue with works of Armin Geertz and Ilkka Pyysiäinen. Though, these scholars hardly mentioned Augustine explicitly in their publications. Hence, a conversation between their written work and the fragments of Augustine requires dialogue of hospitality. I have mentioned tensions between their theories. I also have been struck by similarities and common ground. Geertz and Pyysiäinen studied religion from systematic perspectives. Both focussed on methods in cognitive science of religion and aimed to widen the scope of the discipline towards other scholarly activities that focussed on religion. With the human body in the centre of attention in this book, the choice to discuss embodied aspects of religion was obvious for this chapter.

A leading conclusion from the very journey made in this book is that dialogue *is* a format in *doing* philosophy. Augustine found his inspiration within the tradition of dialogue. Hence, he chose to write dialogues in the period immediately before baptism. Cicero and Plato were major examples for him. He imitated their format. Yet, he transformed their ideas. He made them fit for new challenges. A suggestion from the initiative for dialogue in this book, imperfect as it may be, is that the instrument of dialogue may be as important as tools of analytic philosophy. No criticism on what the hard labour of many scholars has achieved! I admire their meticulous analyses, and profit daily from their painstaking works. They have an aura of objectivity in rationality, and this is, and should be a fundamental part of research on religion. However, dialogue may offer opportunities to include crucial aspects of the human person in all its complexities. A major question is whether my personal contribution as a partner in the dialogue between Augustine and contemporary scholars was a helpful one. Doubtless, it makes this book vulnerable as a scholarly book. Yet, I made clear that this book was not written on topics most urgent in scholarly discussion. The selection of fragments and contemporary theories were motivated by personal motivations, often related to experiences in pastoral work.

The concept of kenosis offered relevant insights. Divine rationality may affect sensible imperfection. Though, in its imperfection, humankind is glorified in the personage of Christ. For me, He is a person. For many others, He represents a personality or personage. Reading Augustine within this perspective suggests a relation of dialogue: the human and the divine Christ. Actually, a horror defeater.

The concept of the *Logos-Sarx* Christology suggested a contrast with kenotic perspectives. Though, we have seen that humility pairs with incarnation. It does not avoid corporeal reality. It includes it. Augustine discussed this topic, incited by Neoplatonic (esoteric) reflections. Yet, he did not reject it completely. He transformed it and made it accessible for the many. So, there is a lot of work to do in future!

Dialogue is bound up in time and persons. Even material factors such as location and space may weigh to a large degree in interpersonal dynamics. Thus, in this specific genre of pragmatic, practical branch of philosophy, there seems to be a promising area for CSR to pursue research on embodied aspects of (philosophical) theology. Patristic authors such as Augustine have left their heritage in the format of written texts. Thus, a hermeneutical theory in CSR may be a promising topic for future interdisciplinary research. It certainly would be in line with Augustine to agree that texts partly represent the material world: embodied thought. However, a major concern is to disclose the highly complex content of analytic philosophical theology to the many, according to Augustine's ideal of accessibility. Obviously, for Augustine, the pulpit was a major opportunity. Though, in our days, and with a more learned audience in mind, probably his dialogues may be relevant for future research in patristics *and* CSR.

Dialogue never represents perfection. They stumble, reiterate, leave important insights aside and stagger over too complex issues. Nevertheless, it is a form of hospitality. Our world needs hospitality. Our world needs dialogue. This book is a grasp for dialogue. It is a personal expression of responsibility.

FURTHER READING

Chapter 1

Davis, St. T. (1983), *Logic and the Nature of God. Library of Philosophy and Religion*, London: Macmillan.

Geertz, A. W. (2004), 'Cognitive Approaches to the Study of Religion', in P. Antes and A. W. Geertz (eds), *Textual, Comparative, Sociological, and Cognitive Approaches: Textual, Comparative, Sociological, and Cognitive Approaches*, 347–99, Berlin: De Gruyter.

Geest, P. van (2011), *The Incomprehensibility of God: Augustine as a Negative Theologian, Late Antique History and Religion, 4*, Leuven: Peeters.

Hadot, P. and A. I. Davidson (1995), *Philosophy as a Way of Life: Spiritual Exercises from Socrates to Foucault*, Malden, MA: Blackwell.

Merricks, T. (2001), *Objects and Persons*, Oxford: Clarendon Press.

Merricks, T. (2009), 'The Resurrection of the Body', in Th. P. Flint and M. C. Rea (eds), *The Oxford Handbook of Philosophical Theology*, 476–90, Oxford: Oxford University Press.

Morris, Th. V. (1986), *The Logic of God Incarnate*, Ithaca: Cornell University Press., reprint 2001, Eugene, Oregon, Wipf and Stock Publishers.

Pyysiäinen, I. (2003), *How Religion Works: Towards a New Cognitive Science of Religion*, Leiden: Brill.

Rea, M. C. and T. Flint, eds. (2009), *Oxford Readings in Philosophical Theology. Volume 1, Trinity, Incarnation, and Atonement*, Oxford: Oxford University Press.

Swinburne, R. (1994), *The Christian God*, Oxford: Clarendon Press.

Taylor, Ch. (2007), *A Secular Age*, Cambridge, MA: Belknap Press of Harvard University Press.

Visala, A. (2011), *Naturalism, Theism and the Cognitive Study of Religion: Religion Explained?* Ashgate Science and Religion Series, Farnham: Ashgate.

Chapter 2

Boersma, G. P. (2016), *Augustine's Early Theology of Image: A Study in the Development of Pro-Nicene Theology. Oxford Studies in Historical Theology*, New York: Oxford University Press.

Brittain, Ch. (2011), 'Augustine as a Reader of Cicero', in R. J. Teske, R. C. Taylor, D. Twetten, and M. Wreen (eds), *Tolle Lege: Essays on Augustine & on Medieval Philosophy in Honor of Roland J. Teske, SJ.*, 81–114, Marquette Studies in Philosophy, 73, Milwaukee, WI: Marquette University Press.

Byers, S. C. (2013), *Perception, Sensibility, and Moral Motivation in Augustine: A Stoic-Platonic Synthesis*, Cambridge: Cambridge University Press.

Daley, B. E. (2018), *God Visible. Patristic Christology Reconsidered. Changing Paradigms in Historical and Systematic Theology*, Oxford: Oxford University Press.

Dupont, A. (2013), *Gratia in Augustine's Sermones Ad Populum during the Pelagian Controversy: Do Different Contexts Furnish Different Insights? Brill's Series in Church History*, Vol. 59, Leiden: Brill.

Adams, M. McCord (1993), 'The Problem of Hell: A Problem of Evil for Christians', in E. Stump (ed.), *Reasoned Faith: Essays in Philosophical Theology in Honor of Norman Kretzmann*, 301–27, Ithaka, London: Cornell University Press.

Chapter 3

Adams, M. McCord (2006), *Christ and Horrors: The Coherence of Christology, Current Issues in Theology*, Cambridge: Cambridge University Press.

Barsalou, L. W, A. K. Barbey, W. K. Simmons and A. Santos (2005), 'Embodiment in Religious Knowledge', *Journal of Cognition and Culture*, 5 (1/2): 14–57.

Davis, St. D., ed (1988), *Encountering Jesus: A Debate on Christology*, Atlanta: John Knox Press.

Lash, N. (1979), in M. Goulder (ed), *Incarnation and Myth: The Debate Continued*, Grand Rapids: Eerdmans, 41–42.

Meconi, D. V. (2013), *The One Christ: St. Augustine's Theology of Deification*, Washington, DC: Catholic University of America Press.

Merricks, T. (2006), 'Split Brains and the Godhead', in Th. Crisp, D. Vander Laan and M. Davidson (eds), *Knowledge and Reality: Essays in Honor of Alvin Plantinga*, 299–326. Dordrecht: Kluwer Academic Publishers.

Nightingale, A. W. (2011), *Once Out of Nature: Augustine on Time and the Body*, Chicago, IL: University of Chicago Press.

Williams, R. D. (2008), 'Augustine's Christology: Its Spirituality and Rhetoric', in P. W. Martens (ed), *In the Shadow of the Incarnation: Essays on Jesus Christ in the Early Church in Honor of Brian E. Daley, S.J.*, 176–89, Notre Dame: University of Notre Dame Press.

Chapter 4

Cameron, M. (2012), *Christ Meets Me Everywhere: Augustine's Early Figurative Exegesis*, Oxford: Oxford University Press.

Czachesz, I. (2014), *The Grotesque Body in Early Christian Discourse: Hell, Scatology and Metamorphosis*, Hoboken: Taylor and Francis.

Davis, St. D., D. Kendall and G. O'Collins, eds. (2002), *The Incarnation: An Interdisciplinary Symposium on the Incarnation of the Son of God*, Oxford: Oxford University Press.

De Smedt, J. and H. De Cruz (2014), 'The Imago Dei as a Work in Progress: A Perspective from Paleoanthropology', *Zygon: Journal of Religion & Science*, 49: 135–56.

Engberg-Pedersen, T. (2007), 'Epilogue', in P. Luomanen, I. Pyysiäinen and R. Uro (eds), *Explaining Christian Origins and Early Judaism: Contributions from Cognitive and Social Science*, 299–311, Leiden: Brill.

Geertz, A. W. (1999), 'Definition as Analytical Strategy in the Study of Religion,' *Historical Reflections/Reflexions Historiques* 25/3: 445–75.

Geertz, A. W. (2000), 'Analytical Theorizing in the Secular Study of Religion', in T. Jensen and M. Rothstein (eds), *Secular Theories on Religion: Current Perspectives*, 21–31, Copenhagen: Museum Tusculanum.

Geertz, A. W. (2008), 'How Not to Do the Cognitive Science of Religion Today', *Method and Theory in the Study of Religion*, 20: 7–21.

Geertz, A. W. (2010), 'Brain, Body and Culture: A Biocultural Theory of Religion', *Method and Theory in the Study of Religion*, 22: 304–21.

Jensen, J. S. (2003), 'Social Facts, Metaphysics, and Rationality in the Human Sciences,' in J. S. Jensen and L. H. Martin (eds), *Rationality and the Study of Religion*, 117–35. London: Routledge.

Pike, K. L. (1971), *Language in Relation to a Unified Theory of the Structure of Human Behaviour*, 2nd rev. ed., Paris: Mouton (1954 1st ed.).

Pyysiäinen, I. (2007), 'The Mystery of the Stolen Body: Exploring Christian Origins', in P. Luomanen, I. Pyysiäinen and R. Uro (eds),

Explaining Christian Origins and Early Judaism: Contributions from Cognitive and Social Science, 57–72, Leiden: Brill.

Pyysiäinen, I. (2015), 'Theism Reconsidered: Belief in God and the Existence of God', *Zygon: Journal of Religion & Science*, 50 (1): 138–50.

Vainio, O. P. (2014), 'Imago Dei and Human Rationality', *Zygon: Journal of Religion & Science* 49: 121–34.

Visala, A. (2014a), 'Imago Dei, Dualism, and Evolution: A Philosophical Defense of the Structural Image of God', *Zygon: Journal of Religion & Science*, 49 (1): 101–20.

Visala, A. (2014b), 'The Evolution of Divine and Human Minds: Evolutionary Psychology, the Cognitive Study of Religion and Theism', in F. Watts and L. Turner (eds), *Evolution, Religion, and Cognitive Science*, 56–73, Oxford: Oxford University Press.

INDEX OF TEXTS

Biblical texts (including partial quotations)

Works of Augustine

INDEX